George Washington Had No Middle Name

STRANGE HISTORICAL FACTS
FROM THE DAYS OF THE
GREEKS AND ROMANS TO THE PRESENT

by Patricia Lee Holt

Citadel Press   *Secaucus, New Jersey*

Published by Citadel Press
A division of Lyle Stuart Inc.
120 Enterprise Avenue, Secaucus, N.J. 07094
In Canada: Musson Book Company
A division of General Publishing Co. Limited
Don Mills, Ontario

Manufactured in the United States of America
10 9 8 7 6 5 4 3 2

Library of Congress Cataloging-in-Publication Data

Holt, Patricia Lee.
    George Washington had no middle name.

    1. History--Miscellanea. 2. History, Military--
Miscellanea. I. Title.
D24.H7 1988   909   87-35801
ISBN 0-8065-1074-9 (pbk.)

For Tommy, Bill, and James

A special thank you to Virginia Christenbury
for all of the encouragement

Why shouldn't truth be stranger than fiction? Fiction, after all, has to make sense.

—MARK TWAIN

Contents

Introduction

Did you know? A war raged for over 300 years between France and England because a king shaved off his beard. Twelve hundred were executed because a general coughed. A famous writer appeared at a public parade naked. Camels were once used by the United States Army to carry supplies. Only one woman in U.S. history was ever awarded the nation's highest award for valor. Another woman joined the Confederate forces during the U.S. Civil War, raised a company of cavalry and equipped it at her own expense. Just as amazing is the fact she disguised herself as a man, going so far as to wear a false beard and mustache!

These are just a few of the unusual historical facts that I discovered when researching this book. History fascinates me, although this has not always been the case. It was easy for me to daydream when a teacher lectured on most any aspect of U.S. or world history. "Learn the dates, they are of utmost importance," the instructor would say. And I, along with many of my classmates, moaned.

I've never been good at memorizing numbers. There are times when I have to think for a few moments in order to recite my own telephone number. There were so many dates emphasized in my history classes that I found myself scribbling every one of them on paper. As a result, what should have been a fascinating subject was instead tedious and uninteresting.

The germ of the idea for this book came about as the result of a disagreement with a friend. She informed me that Theodore Roosevelt was the youngest man to become President of the United States. I of course knew that I was far from being an historian. Yet I was positive that my friend was wrong. The first President I remembered well was John F. Kennedy, and I was positive that he was the youngest man ever to become President.

The next day I visited the main public library and looked up Theodore Roosevel in the encyclopedia. To my astonishment I realized that my friend had been correct. I learned that Theodore Roosevelt was the youngest man ever to become President. He took office at the age of 42. Roosevelt had been Vice-President for only six months when President William McKinley was assassinated in September 1901. With further research I discovered that John F. Kennedy was the youngest man ever elected President. The key words were "become," and "elected."

I thought of myself as a person with at least average intelligence, and wondered why I had not been aware of that Presidential fact. I also wondered if most other people were aware of it.

I had been interested in reading about little-known historical facts for several years, and could hold my own in a game of Trivial Pursuit. Yet, I was not even aware of the fact I had just discovered, and it was not just a "trivial" bit of knowledge either.

While reading books on unusual facts, I had learned that fleas can jump one hundred times their own height—a feat comparable to a man's jumping as high as a forty-story building (the little rascals could even outjump Superman). I also learned that a termite queen can live for more than fifty years. And a healthy queen can produce over thirty thousand eggs in only one day. That meant a queen termite could conceivably give birth to about half a billion children. Now, I realized that my assimilation of this type of trivial information was of no real consequence to me, unless of course I ultimately decided to join the ranks of the Orkin exterminators.

I spent several more hours in the library that day, and discovered several historical items of which I was unaware. Facts that I felt most people did not know. And the more I researched the more interested I became, finally deciding that I would try to write a book composed entirely of historical facts that most people did not know.

Historical facts do not have to be boring. Many are interesting, entertaining, fascinating and even humorous. But this kind of historical information is not in ordinary history books.

What's even more amazing: many historical "facts" a lot of us believe are factual are *not*. For example: Teddy Roosevelt and his Rough Riders charged up San Juan Hill on horses. There is a Congressional Medal of Honor. The Romans used chariots for war. Gun powder was invented by Chinese firecracker makers. The first major engagement of the Revolutionary War was at Bunker Hill. Paul Revere's ride was the most perilous and important ride in the Revolutionary War.

Betsy Ross designed the American Flag. The term "damned Yankee" was coined by the Confederates during the U.S. Civil War. The Battle of New Orleans was fought during the War of 1812. The famous Bowie knife was invented by James Bowie. In 1862, the Battle of Shiloh was fought at a town called Shiloh. General George Armstrong Custer fought at the battle of the Little Big Horn . . . These are all facts. Right? Wrong!

This book will tell the truth about these fallacies and others. And there are articles on strange occurrences; odd ball characters—the well-known and the obscure; "shady" facts about some 'respected' heroes, articles on heroines history books never mention, and much more.

There are facts that will make you smile. Some will surprise or even shock. My purpose has been to inform as well as entertain. And to try to make these unusual history facts as interesting for you to read as they were for me to research and compile.

You may begin your quest for fascinating facts on page one and read right through to the last item in the book. Or you can start with the category of special interest to you and then skip around.

I believe that after reading this book, you, like me, will agree that truth is indeed stranger than fiction.

—PATRICIA LEE HOLT

Greek and Roman Days

A STICKY SITUATION

The advancing armies of Pompey the Great discovered great tubs of azalea honey left behind by Spaniards. Delighted with the sticky treat, the army immediately began to stuff themselves with honey. After devouring the entire booty, most of the men became deathly ill because of the toxic impurities in the honey. The patient Spaniards, who had been waiting in the hills, then swooped down and crushed the disabled legions.

* * *

SOLAR POWER

A powerful Roman force attacked the city of Syracuse in 214 B.C. Syracuse was the home of the great mathematician and astronomer, Archimedes. The Greek inventor devised one ingenious weapon after another to hold off the Roman legions. Among the weapons Archimedes devised was the catapult, which sent a ton of stones flying as far as 600 feet.

But Archimedes' most brilliant contraption was an arrangement of mirrors that directed the concentrated rays of the sun on the Roman ships and set them ablaze.

* * *

SAVED BY A CLEAN SHAVE

Alexander the Great ordered his entire army to shave their heads and faces. His premise was that beards and long hair gave the enemy a distinct advantage, making it easier to grab his men in order to cut off their heads.

* * *

HANNIBAL'S HOT ROCKS

When Hannibal invaded Italy, in the third century B.C., the agents fire and vinegar were used to smash a path through the alps. Hannibal's engineers heated immovable rocks with blazing logs, then poured vinegar over the rocks. The rocks split into small pieces and could then be pushed aside.

* * *

ALEXANDER LOVED A PARADE

Alexander, the greatest of generals, devised a brilliant plan to defeat Glaucias and his wild Taulantians in his Balkan and Illyrian campaigns of 335 B.C. The problem was how to draw the enemy from their secure position in the hills down into the plains where the superior discipline of Alexander's troops would defeat them. So he held a parade! He ordered his cavalry and infantry to perform a battle drill, secure in the knowledge that there were few events more likely to draw a crowd than a military spectacle. Enthralled, the Taulantians began to assemble on the lower slopes of the foothills for a closer view. When they became captivated at the spectacle, Alexander gave the order to attack. Raising a frightening cheer, clanging their spears on their shields, Alexander's infantry rushed and routed their startled audience.

* * *

RUN, PHEIDIPPIDES, RUN!

Pheidippides was the best runner in Athens. In September of 490 B.C., King Darius, the ruler of the powerful Persian empire, sent his army to attack the plain of Marathon, just a few miles from Athens.

The Athenians were greatly outnumbered but marched out to meet the invaders. Pheidippides was sent to deliver a request for help to the Athenian's allies in Sparta.

Racing out of the city on foot, he forged ahead across rough, rocky terrain, running all day and through the night. He arrived in Sparta the next morning having covered a distance of 140 miles. Pheidippides delivered his message and getting the answer, he ran back to join the Athenian troops, again covering the distance in a day and a night.

The Athenian and Persian armies clashed in the now famous battle of Marathon, a few days after Pheidippides' return. He fought in the battle as an infantryman even though he'd had only a short time to rest after his grueling two-way run.

Against all odds the Athenians defeated the Persians. Pheidippides was exhausted when the fighting ended.

Casting his heavy armor off, he accepted the Athenian Commander's request to carry news of the victory to Athens.

Pheidippides covered the 22 miles 1,470 yards from Marathon to Athens in just a few hours. But the ordeal was too much for his already overtaxed system. With his last breaths, he shouted, "Victory, victory," as he staggered into the central marketplace of Athens, then dropped to the pavement, dead.

Pheidippides' noble patriotic deed was never forgotten. In the years that followed the Athenians established a series of memorial games, including running events of all kinds. A road-race called the marathon was made a regular event, when the Olympic Games were revived in 1896. In 1924, its distance was standardized at 26 miles 385 yards.

* * *

THE WARS ARE OVER

A first-century Roman soldier and administrator, Frontinus, claimed he would ignore all new developments in war machinery. He wrote a book stating the invention of engines of war had "long since reached its limit," and could not be improved upon.

* * *

BEN HUR'S LOSS

The Romans did not use chariots for war—their chariots were used for sport and transportation.

* * *

ARMOR MAKES THE MAN

In the great Roman army, military garb as well as role was once determined by wealth. Shield, breastplate, greaves (armor for the leg below the knee), helmet, and sword and spear was the uniform of the day for the richest men. The less wealthy men did not wear breastplates. The poorest men carried only spear and sword and wore no armor.

* * *

FOLLOW THE SIGN

Constantine suddenly had a vision of a cross in the sky, complete with the words "By this sign you will conquer," in the midst of a crucial battle against the barbarians in A.D. 312.

Constantine was victorious in the battle and consequently adopted the new faith, which was still struggling to survive in the Roman Empire. Christianity soon became the official religion of the Roman world and its future was assured.

* * *

NERO THE BAD

A lot of bad can be said of Nero, most of which is true; it is also true that he disliked the spectacle of violent death. He built a wooden amphitheater in A.D. 57, ruling that no gladiators, not even condemned criminals, were to be killed in any of the games presented. Actually, the gladiators were to engage in fencing matches.

The taste for blood among Roman spectators prevailed and Nero could not make his policy stick. He bowed to public pressure and later "games" presented in Nero's reign were indeed bloody.

* * *

THE LOSS WAS TO THE ENEMY

The Byzantine emperor Constantine V and his army of 80,000 men lined up against a Bulgarian army of 80,000 in A.D. 743. Constantine won an amazing victory. There were no casualties from his army, and not a single soldier was even wounded. Twenty thousand men were lost by the Bulgarians.

* * *

DREAM COME TRUE

A meek soldier named Romanus dreamed in 1065 that he was sitting at the side of the Byzantine empress Eudokia. After telling his dream to a guard, he was arrested and sentenced to death, but the empress pardoned him.

Two years later, when Emperor Constantine X died, Eudokia married the soldier—and he became Emperor Romanus IV, just as in his dream.

* * *

THE ARAB MOLLY PITCHER

The Arabs produced a "Molly Pitcher" during the Crusades. The wife of an archer who was killed at the Battle of Damascus picked up his bow and immediately joined the conflict. The soldier's widow hit the Crusaders' standardbearer with one arrow and the commander with another. More than pride was wounded; her act damaged the Crusaders' morale and contributed to the Arab victory.

* * *

THE FIRST TANK

The first military tank was used by Count Jan Žižka, leader of the Protestant Hussites of Bohemia. Sigismund, the German King and nominal head of the Holy Roman Empire, invaded Bohemia in 1420. Žižka was waiting with his wagon fort, a heavy, horse-drawn farm wagon covered with sheets of iron. The crew fired crossbows and guns through loopholes pierced in the side.

Žižka's tactics were creative and original. His wagon forts were slow and cumbersome, so his strategy was to force the enemy to attack at a disadvantage. Žižka used the wagon forts in much the same way that modern generals deploy their tanks. The wagon forts were dug in behind a ditch and linked together by chains making a formidable obstacle to any advance.

Žižka was victorious with a mere 25,000 men, crushing Sigismund's invasion force of more than 100,000. The Hussites demolished their enemy for the next 14 years. Yet despite the success of mobile artillery, it was not reintroduced until 200 years later by the King of Sweden.

Around the World

EXCUSE MY TRUNK

Elephants on both sides were used to fight in only one battle in history. In the Fourth Syrian War, in 217 B.C., Antiochus III of Syria used Asian elephants when he attacked Ptolemy IV's Egyptian army with its smaller elephants (which are now extinct). The larger Asian elephants were the victors, but the Egyptian army went on to win a celebrated victory in the engagement at Raphia on the Egyptian border.

* * *

ANY LENGTH TO WIN A WAR

A 24-foot-long pike called a sarissa was employed as a weapon by the famous Macedonian Phalanx. The sarissa permitted a warrior in the sixth fighting rank to extend his weapon to the first. This weapon was not subsequently employed by other peoples.

* * *

THE BATTLE WAS THE CATS MEOW

According to legend, cats led to the defeat of the Egyptian army in 525 B.C.

The Persian invader Cambyses put a row of cats—which the Egyptians considered sacred—in front of his troops. And the Egyptian archers refused to shoot their arrows at the venerated animals.

* * *

HOT GRENADES

In the tenth century, conquering Arab armies used a primitive form of flame thrower and hand grenade. Flames of niter and sulfur spurted through copper tubes. Terra cotta was used to fashion grenades shaped to fit the contours of the hand. The grenades were filled with inflammable naphtha, and covered with relief designs to prevent them from slipping when being thrown.

* * *

SOLDIER-EXECUTIONERS

Genghis Khan killed 1,748,000 at Nishapur in 1221, in only an hour.

After every battle soldiers in Genghis Khan's army became executioners. The people of a defeated town were ordered to assemble outside the walls of the town. Each Mongol soldier was ordered to kill at least fifty of the captives. Armed with battle axes, the soldiers cut an ear off every victim, collected the ears in a sack and took them to their officers to be counted to prove they'd carried out orders.

* * *

SHE HELPED CAPTURE THE CRUSADERS

A woman ruled in Medieval Egypt and planned the attack against Louis IX and his Crusaders. Shajar-Al-burr kept the death of her husband, the Sultan, a secret when he died during the siege of Cairo. She gave orders in his name and devised the strategy of cutting the Crusaders' supply lines. Her strategy helped the Egyptians win the battle and led to the capture of Louis IX, in 1250.

* * *

A BEASTLY BATTLE

In the thirteenth century Genghis Khan planned a clever ruse against the Chinese city of Volohai. Unable to take the fortress by storm, the commander ordered his men to trap all the cats and swallows in the vicinity. Tufts of cotton were tied to the tails of the beasts and then set on fire. The cats and birds were then turned loose. Immediately the terrified swallows flew into the air and headed for their nests in the city, while the angry cats sped home for their lairs. A few of the felines and fowl perished enroute, a few were killed by the citizens of Volohai, but most got home and set the city blazing in a thousand places. While the population were busy furiously fighting the fires, Genghis Khan and his warriors entered the city.

* * *

NOTHING TO LOSE YOUR HEAD OVER

In the late fourteenth century, when the fortress of the knights of St. John in Smyrna was attacked by the legions of the Mongol conqueror Timur, a large reserve fleet of ships arrived to aid the besieged garrison. In response, Timur ordered that the heads of the knights already slain be loaded into a giant catapult and fired at the arriving ships. As soon as the onslaught began, the reserve fleet raised their sails, turned around, and sailed away, leaving the knights to fend for themselves.

* * *

THE FIRST USE OF GUNPOWDER

Weaponry was revolutionized by the invention of gunpowder—usually attributed to the Chinese firecracker makers of the 9th century. But in actuality, gunpowder was first introduced in Europe in the 1300's. Cannons and field artillery were first used by the Dutch.

* * *

A FISHY BATTLE

A battle was fought near Orléans France on February 12, 1429, between the French under the Duke of Bourbon, and the English, commanded by Sir John Fastolfe. The English achieved victory by aborting the attempt of the French to intercept and capture a convoy of salted herrings on its way from Paris to the English forces besieging Orléans.

* * *

WAR OF THE WHISKERS

Bearded King Louis VII of France married Eleanor, daughter of a French duke. King Louis VII shaved off his beard on his way home from the Crusades. Eleanor was extremely upset when Louis returned home and said he looked ugly without his beard. He refused to grow his whiskers back, so Eleanor divorced him and married King Henry II of England. Eleanor demanded the return of her dowry of two provinces but King Louis refused. King Henry declared war to regain the dowry by force.

The war between France and England raged for 301 years and peace was finally declared in 1453, after the Battle of Roven.

* * *

TANKS AND AIRCRAFT DESIGNED 500 YEARS AGO

The many-sided genius of the fifteenth-century artist and engineer Leonardo da Vince produced schemes for a large number of modern inventions, hundreds of years before their time—including road vehicles, aircraft, and weapons.

Leonardo's military designs included a tank with sloping sides to shield it from artillery, a rapid-firing gun, exploding shot, and a giant crossbow. He even proposed stench bombs to be shot by a bow or catapult.

He turned out the first known design for a parachute, something like a square tent, and worked on several plans for flying machines.

His designs for a ship of the air included a vertical takeoff aircraft, using an aerial screw similar to the modern rotor of a helicopter. Still another showed a retractable landing gear.

Leonardo lacked the temperament to carry through most of his schemes.

He died with his plans unpublished, leaving his ideas to be rediscovered by others—often hundreds of years later.

* * *

THE TURKS' FANTASTIC WEAPON

A gun of hooped iron that had to be pulled by oxen and maneuvered by a hundred men was used by the Turks to terrorize their enemies in the fifteenth century. The gun fired half-ton stone balls.

* * *

WATCH THAT YO-YO!

In the sixteenth century, the Yo-Yo originated as a weapon in the Philippine Islands. It weighed four pounds and had a 20-foot cord. The Yo-Yo was introduced to America in 1929 by Louis Marx, the toymaker.

* * *

SHORT SUBJECT

Jeffrey Hudson, a dwarf eighteen inches high, served as a captain of cavalry in the British army. Hudson lived from 1619 to 1682. He made his first public appearance inside a pie served at the table of the Duke of Buckingham. When he was about thirty years old, he "shot up" in size, attaining the height of three feet, nine inches.

* * *

A HERO LEG

In 1644, Peter Stuyvesant, who later became the Dutch colonial governor of New Amsterdam (New York), sustained a wound in the leg in battle against the Portuguese in the Caribbean. The leg had to be amputated in Holland. The Dutch granted the severed limb a Christian burial with full military honors.

* * *

BEAT MY BROOM

Martin Harpertzoon Tromp, a Dutch admiral and victor in 33 sea fights, is said to have tied a broom to the masthead of his flagship after he defeated the English admiral Robert Blake in 1652 at the battle of Dungeness, and then sailed triumphantly through the English Channel in token of his having made a clean sweep of the seas.

The English admiral in charge of the British fleet is said to have tied a horsewhip to his masthead to symbolize his determination to give Tromp a good thrashing. The flying streamer or pennant flown on British men-of-war is believed to be derived from Blake's horsewhip.

* * *

SOLDIER FOR ALL SEASONS

Jean Theurel died in 1807 at the age of 123. Theurel served as a soldier in three centuries, first as a lad of fifteen. In 1699 he joined the Touraine Regiment to defend France's honor in the war against Holland. He fought bravely in hundreds of battles, and in later years joined up with the First Company of Paris. In 1777, Theurel was finally promoted to captain by Louis XVI. At the time the King tactfully suggested that since Theurel was now 92, he might consider retirement.

Theurel did not retire and continued to live in the First Company barracks, remaining on the active rolls. His tenure was not challenged again until 1801, when Napoleon learned of his status. Theurel was officially deactivated and given a pension of 1,500 francs at the age of 118.

* * *

MONKEY BUSINESS

In 1705 Britain was at war with France. One morning on the beach of West Hartlepool, England, the villagers watched in amazement as a hairy stranger climbed out of a rowboat. The odd-looking creature jabbered unintelligibly. The stranger was actually an ape, previously the mascot of a wrecked ship. The villagers weren't at all familiar with apes. They court-martialed the beast, found it guilty, and hanged it as a French spy.

* * *

EARMARKED FOR WAR

In 1738, Captain Robert Jenkins displayed a peculiar specimen before a Parliamentary committee in London. The astonished parliament gazed in horror at a human ear pickled in brine. Jenkins identified the ear as his own, charging that it had been cut off while he was sailing in the West Indies. Appalled, the British declared war on Spain. The war became known as the War of Jenkins' Ear, which expanded into the War of the Austrian Succession.

* * *

WAR BABY

During the French Revolution, Richeborg, a dwarf, was employed as a secret agent. Twenty-three inches high at maturity, he was disguised as an infant and wrapped in swaddling clothes. Richeborg carried crucial secret dispatches while being taken in and out of Paris in the arms of his "nurse." He died in Paris at nearly one hundred years of age.

* * *

LOVE FOR SAIL

The Tahitian Islands were discovered in 1767 by Captain Samuel Wallis. Not long after, the crew of his ship, the *Dolphin*, made their own exciting discovery. In exchange for iron nails that held the *Dolphin* together, the island girls offered hours of sex. The nails were needed to make fishhooks.

The crew ignored commands from Wallis to stop the trading. In a short while the *Dolphin* was literally falling apart at the seams due to pilferage of nails. Soon the Tahitians began to demand longer nails (the most luscious girls could only be had for the longest nails). Finally Wallis refused to grant shore leave until the guilty parties confessed. None of the men wanted to admit guilt and blamed a Mr. Pinckney (his dislodging of nails had caused the ship's mainsail to collapse). He was flogged, and shore leave was ended.

The Tahitians were confused about the entire incident. They said they'd been led to believe that it was customary among white people to fornicate freely and openly, and that it was the white man's way of saying, "Hello."

* * *

SHE FOUGHT IN 200 BATTLES

During the French Revolution of 1789, many people remained faithful to the King. The people of Vendéen in western France refused to side with the rebels. In 1793, they rose against the revolutionary regime and fought for six years to restore the Bourbons to the throne.

Renée Bordereau, called "The Second Joan of Arc," became the great heroine of the revolt. Her father was killed before her eyes by revolutionary soldiers, and she enlisted in the Vendéean army at the age of 23.

Dressing as a male soldier, she always led attacks and sought the most dangerous posts. Renée's courage was greatly admired by her fellow soldiers, and they never suspected she was a woman.

Napoleon feared Renée would lead a new rebellion even after he put down the Vendéean revolt. He put a bounty of 40 million francs on her head. She was captured and Napoleon had her put in a prison for five years.

In 1815, two years after the final overthrow of Napoleon, Renée Bordereau was received with honors at the court of the French King, Louis XVIII.

* * *

HOIST BY HIS OWN PETARD

General Henry Shrapnel invented shrapnel. He was also the first man wounded by his idea. It happened in a premature explosion at the 1793 evacuation of Dunkirk during the French revolutionary wars.

* * *

THE FIRST PRISONER-OF-WAR CAMP

The first prisoner-of-war camp was built in Britain. Norman Cross Depot, near Stilton in Huntingdonshire, was erected by HM Transport Commissioners for the reception of French POW's. Norman Cross Depot was occupied for the first time on April 7, 1797. POW's had previously been confined in civil prisons, fortresses or floating hulks. The number of prisoners entering Britain had grown so large by the end of 1796 that it became necessary to provide special accommodations. The 40-acre camp was constructed in less than four months and was designed to house 8,000 prisoners.

Three hundred sailors from the warships *Reunion* and *Revolutionaire* were the first batch of prisoners to arrive at the camp. Attempts to escape were relatively frequent, but seldom successful. Prisoners who attempted to escape were punished by so many days in the "Black Hole." Rewards payable to the captors had to be defrayed by the prisoner himself, who was put on half rations until the debt was paid off.

Norman Cross Depot was closed in 1802, when peace was declared. It was reopened in 1803 with the renewal of hostilities and continued in operation until 1814.

Some POW's remained in captivity from 1797 until the camp's demolition in 1816. This record is surpassed only by the last German POW's of World War II, who remained captive in Soviet Russia nearly 20 years after the end of the war.

* * *

A DEADLY COUGH

Napoleon coughed and 1,200 people died.

In 1799 he was a general in the Middle East and had just decided to release his prisoners. Then came the deadly cough. Napoleon exclaimed "Ma sacrée Toux" (My confounded cough). His officers thought he said, "Massacrez Tous" (Kill them all), and they executed 1,200 prisoners.

* * *

NAPOLEON'S SUPER WEAPON

Napoleon used a semaphore telegraph—visual messages from as far as the eye could see—to gain an enormous advantage over his enemies. A message could be sent from Paris to Rome in only four hours.

* * *

NAPOLEON NEVER MET HIS WATERLOO

Since June 1815, the name "Waterloo" has been synonymous with ultimate defeat. Britain's Duke of Wellington ended Napoleon's imperial ambitions, but the famous battle did not happen at Waterloo; but rather at a small valley to Waterloo's south in the hamlet of La Haie Sainte.

The town of Waterloo seems to have claimed the site for Napoleon's defeat because Wellington slept there before the battle, or perhaps because he went there to write the news home shortly after the victory.

*   *   *

SAVE THE LANDLORDS

When rifle sights were first provided to the British Army during the Napoleonic Wars, an officer commanding Irish troops tried to reject them because, he said, if his men were given them, every English landlord in Ireland would be dead in two weeks.

*   *   *

NAPOLEON'S TURNABOUT

A young soldier had been expelled from the army and was disgraced, despondent, and suicidal by the age of twenty-five. The soldier was Napoleon. In a complete turnabout, just one year later he became the youngest general in the French army and began winning victories with ragged troops who were at the point of starvation.

*   *   *

O'HIGGINS'S ARMY OF ANIMALS

Bernardo O'Higgins lead a small army of Chilean patriots who had been trying to gain freedom from Spanish rule since 1810. The Chileans fought bravely against the Spanish, even though their army was much smaller and had few weapons.

The Spanish king sent boatloads of soldiers to wipe out O'Higgins and his patriot army. The Chileans fought long and hard, but under constant onslaught, and worn out by fighting, thirst and merciless heat, they stood surrounded.

On October 2, 1814, O'Higgins was struck by an enemy bullet. The Chilean patriots seemed doomed to defeat, when the wounded O'Higgins conceived a plan. He ordered his men to round up as many cows, sheep, dogs and mules as possible.

Once the vast array of animals was assembled before him, O'Higgins was lifted to his horse. With a shout and sharp lash of his whip, O'Higgins sent his steed charging ahead. The mass display of frightened animals became a bellowing, stampeding mass. Defiantly O'Higgins drove them on—straight toward the Spanish lines. Maddened by fear, the frenzied animals paid no heed to the formidable array of soldiers before them.

Terrified, the Spanish veterans broke ranks and ran at the sight of the thundering herd of animals.

O'Higgins and his men galloped through the path the animals had made for them. Slashing with their swords, they sped through the Spanish lines.

Before the Spaniards could reorganize their forces, the Chileans were safe in the mountains where they recuperated, enlisted new recruits and gathered arms.

Bernardo O'Higgins returned three years later, as the head of an army of 4,000 men to destroy the Spanish battalions. In 1818, O'Higgins proudly proclaimed Chile's independence from Spain, and became the first ruler of the new nation.

* * *

PASS THE CHEESE, PLEASE

The Uruguayan navy once fought a sea battle using cheese as cannonballs.

In the 1840's, Argentine dictator Juan Manuel de Rosas ordered his navy to blockade Montevideo, the capitol of Uruguay. The Uruguayans put up a strong fight, until they ran out of ammunition. Desperate, they raided the galleys of their ships and loaded their cannons with aged, hard Edam cheeses and fired them at the surprised enemy.

The Uruguayans were victors in the "cheezy" battle.

* * *

GREASE STARTED THE REBELLION

Grease started the Scopy Rebellion, an uprising of colonial troops in India between 1857 and 1858. Some newly issued cartridges for the regulation Enfield rifles were rumored to be greased with pig and cow fat. A mutiny ensued among Hindu and Moslem soldiers. Rifle shells had to be uncapped in one's mouth at the time. The mutineers believed that this was a mortal sin, because it violated their religious dietary law against eating pork and beef.

* * *

SHE DISGUISED HERSELF AS A MAN FOR OVER 50 YEARS

Dr. James Barry was probably the first woman to attend the University of Edinburgh Medical School. The one thing known for certain about Dr. Barry's identity is the date of *her*, not his, death—July 25, 1865.

Dr. Barry was an inspector surgeon general in the British Army, and served as a colonial medical inspector in South Africa and elsewhere in the British Empire for over 50 years.

She was not suspected of being a woman until her death in 1865. When a charwoman was called in to lay out the 71-year-old physician's body, it was discovered that the sex of the corpse was that of a female! Moreover she had at some time given birth to a child.

Students who remembered Dr. Barry when she was a student at Edinburgh University in 1808, could tell very little that shed any light on the strange masquerade. They recalled that she was small and rather effeminate in appearance.

She was remembered as an excellent student, a hard worker, and not fond of mixing with others. When she qualified as a doctor, she could have easily gone into practice in Edinburgh or elsewhere without being in constant fear of having her false identity exposed.

Instead, for some incomprehensible reason, she enlisted in the army, where there was always the possibility of her true sex being revealed. In those days there were few competent doctors who would accept service in the British army, and all Dr. Barry had to do was sign the forms and don uniform.

Dr. Barry was conscientious in a time when soldiers were often viewed as the scum of the earth and were treated callously. She sent outspoken reports and complaints about conditions in all military and leper hospitals. The reports were long and bitter and, as the authorities reluctantly realized eventually, completely justified.

Dr. Barry had performed one of the first successful caesarean sections of modern times in 1862. Not only had she achieved a reputation of extraordinary surgical skill, but she was also renowned as an expert duelist. She fought at least three duels and in one confrontation wounded her opponent, Captain Cloete, so seriously that she was sent home for court-martial.

Despite the rigorous duty of military service, Dr. Barry became a persistent opponent of the practice of allowing anyone to set up in business as a druggist or dispenser without any training. Because of her adamant fight for this cause, it is largely due to those efforts that all druggists are now properly trained and examined.

The mystery of Dr. James Barry's true identity, and the motives for her strange masquerade, has never been solved. For over 50 years she had lived as a man among men and been accepted as one without ever arousing more than a faint suspicion. She was buried with full military honors at the cemetery at Kensal Green, in London, in July 1865.

* * *

THE WORLD'S MOST COSTLY WAR

The most costly war in terms of human life, in all

history, was called by those who fought in it "The Great Peace."

Between 1850 and 1864, twenty million people were killed in this war and, while the Chinese fought amongst themselves, European powers, notably Britain, France and Russia, took full advantage to extract by force, or threats of force, commercial and territorial concessions.

It was the use of this force, costing thousands of Chinese and European lives, which is remembered now by both sides rather than the events which began the war. In 1850, Hung Hsiu Chuan announced that he was the youngest brother of Jesus Christ and was going to reform the land and right the many wrongs in China. Hung and his three brothers, known as "the Four Hung Princes," destroyed their private property, gave all their goods away and attracted a great following. Hung's first army was described by its enemies as "Ten Thousand Long-Haired Bandits," because they were forbidden to cut their hair. They proclaimed the abolition of prostitution, the binding of women's feet, the sale of slaves, opium smoking, adultery, gambling, witchcraft and the use of tobacco and wine.

In the cause of these reforms thousands upon thousands were slaughtered without mercy.

Hung's armies carried his influence far and wide even after his puritanical rule was dissipated. In 1853 he proclaimed himself Emperor Tien Wang and is said to have lived a carefree existence in the seclusion of his palace attended by numerous concubines.

*   *   *

CHINA'S FEMALE SOLDIERS

When the Tae-Ping Rebellion in China broke out in 1850, women as well as men rendered military service.

In 1853 in the city of Nanking, an army of 500,000 women—recruited from various parts of the Chinese Empire—was organized and divided into brigades of 13,000 each, under female officers. Ten thousand of these women were specially selected for garrison-duty in the city. The rest performed the drudgery of the ordinary soldier's life—digging trenches, throwing up earthworks, and planting artillery batteries. The Tae-Ping rebellion was not suppressed until 1864.

* * *

A HURRICANE STOPPED THE WAR

In 1888, Otto von Bismark, the ruler of Germany, wanted to establish a German colony in Samoa, a group of islands in the South Pacific Ocean. A Germany naval fleet was sent to Samoa to shell native villages. German shells destroyed American property in Samoa, and German sailors later ripped down an American flag.

The United States sent a fleet of warships to the island to protect the Americans there. The American and German warships faced each other ready to fire at each other in a Samoan harbor. Suddenly a devastating hurricane struck the islands and destroyed both fleets. German and American sailors rallied to each others' aid in order to survive the disaster, and the grievances between the two countries were soon forgotten. Had it not been for the intervention of a hurricane, the United States and Germany might have gone to war that year.

* * *

THE SHORTEST WAR

The shortest war on record was fought between Zanzibar and England in 1896. From the beginning of hostilities to the surrender of Zanzibar by Sultan Said Khalid, there elapsed only 38 minutes.

* * *

CLOTHES MAKE THE KING

The national anthem of Great Britain is "God Save the King." It was played 16 or 17 times without stopping on the morning of February 9, 1909, by a German military band on the platform of Rathenau Railway Station, in Brandenburg, Germany. The reason for the continuous playing was that King Edward VII of England—the man whom they were to welcome—was inside a railway car. The king was having a difficult time getting dressed and while he struggled to get into a military uniform, the band played on and on and on.

* * *

WHAT'S YOUR NAME

Jean Castle, a 15-year-old French youth, fell and developed total amnesia while fleeing from German soldiers in the Great war in 1915. Nine years later and still unable to remember any of his past, Castle met a lovely English girl and fell in love with her. When the young girl told him her name—also Jean Castle—his amnesia vanished and he totally recovered his memory.

* * *

AN ISLAND SPORT

Karate did not come to Japan until 1916. The martial art was practiced solely by the Okinawan islanders prior to this time. The Okinawans developed it centuries earlier as a means of weaponless defense against the Japanese.

* * *

KITTY KAT PILOTS

Russian scientists looked into the possibility of training cats to pilot air-to-air missiles in 1970. Their research was supposed to be based on B.F. Skinner's proposal to use pigeons as bombardiers, which the noted behaviorist had offered to the United States Navy during World War II. Skinner had noted that felines get airsick quite easily. Aware of this complication, the Soviet researchers considered using the severed brain of a cat in the pilot's seat rather than the whole animal.

* * *

YOUNGEST SOLDIERS

President Francisco Nguema of Equatorial Guinea decreed in March 1976 compulsory military service for all boys between the ages of 7 and 14. Any parent refusing to hand over his or her son "will be imprisoned or shot."

The youngest soldier to enlist in the twentieth century was probably William Frederick Price (b. June 1, 1891), who enlisted in the British Army at Aldershot,

May 23, 1903, aged 11 years 365 days.

* * *

IRAN'S CHILD SOLDIERS

As of this writing, Iran and Iraq have been at war for four years. Among the "troops" confronting the Iraqi arsenal are hundreds of Iranian children (ages 12 to 17). Terrance Smith, in *The New York Times Magazine*, tells of an East European journalist, a reluctant eyewitness "who could hardly believe what he was seeing: '. . . tens of thousands,' of children 'roped together, in groups of 20 to prevent the fainthearted from deserting, hurl themselves onto barbed wire or march into the Iraqi minefields in the face of withering machine gun fire to clear the way for Iranian tanks.'

" 'We have so few tanks,' an Iranian officer explained, without apology.

The parents of the children were promised that if their sons were killed, they would be granted small amounts of money, an increase in rations, an assortment of other benefits and a line on their identity cards indicating that the family had a martyr.

The children go off to camps for intense brainwashing, a smattering of military training. Trained to die, each is given a headband with a religious slogan, a khaki-colored rough jacket with the stenciled message that they have "permission of the Imam (Khomeini) to enter heaven," and a key on a chain around their necks to ensure their entry.

An Iranian woman living in exile has made three trips to Iraq to interview the survivors. After speaking with nearly 200, she estimated that for each boy who makes it to a prison camp, 99 are blown to bits by mines or machine-gunned to death.

* * *

WHERE'S THE BOMB?

Zinaida Bragantsova, of Moscow, had been telling people for 43 years that a World War II bomb was buried under her bed. Finally, in 1984, someone took her seriously, and demolition experts found it and blew it up.

Zinaida finally got rid of the bomb, but lost her house.

According to the Soviet newspaper *Literary Gazette,* Zinaida told authorities that the bomb crashed through the roof of her house in Berdyansk in 1941, when Nazi troops advanced toward the Ukranian city.

"Where's your bomb, Grandma?" asked the smiling army lieutenant sent to talk to Zinaida. "No doubt, under your bed?"

"Under my bed," Zinaida, 74, answered dryly.

Zinaida's home was destroyed when experts exploded the bomb. But, *Literary Gazette* said, "The grandmother, freed of her bomb, will soon receive a new apartment."

* * *

JUMPING WITH A SONG IN HIS HEART

British Army Sergeant Hector Macmillian made a leap from an airplane to commemorate his 700th parachute jump. Macmillian, dressed in full Scottish national dress, including kilts, played *The Road to the Isles* on his bagpipes as he descended.

* * *

PEACENIKS

The nations of Iceland, Costa Rica and Liechtenstein have no armed forces.

* * *

EUROPE'S DRAFT-DODGERS

In the last 25 years, West Germany has generated the largest number of conscientious objectors among the democracies of Europe. More than 200,000 Germans have pulled "community service" since 1961. By working in various welfare organizations and hospitals, the conscientious objectors have a legal alternative to compulsory service in the armed forces, the Bundeswehr.

Conscientious objectors must perform two years of community service in lieu of 18 months of military service.

In 1984, about 10,000 West Germans—unwilling to become conscripts—moved to West Berlin in an effort to avoid military or community service where no such duty is required of permanent residents.

The number of "draft-dodgers" in West Berlin is estimated by authorities to be 45,000. They can remain until age 28, and then return to West Germany without fear of being called up.

* * *

REMINDERS OF WAR

Although the Swedes have not been at war since 1814, they were once the most bellicose and successful warriors in Europe. Consequently, Sweden owns some 3,500 captured battle flags, the largest collection in existence.

* * *

AN ARMY LIKE NO OTHER

The Netherlands has an army like no other in the world. Recently it became the first fully unionized fighting force in the world. The union, known as the VVDM, has made some radical changes in military life.

For one thing the look of the Dutch Army is decidedly different. There are few close-cropped haircuts among the troops. The union insists that the men have the right to wear their hair in any manner they choose. But long-haired men must wear hairnets when operating heavy machinery. When on maneuvers, most men wear sneakers instead of cumbersome combat boots.

The respectful gesture of saluting is frowned upon by the union—"a strange way of contact between people"—and this primeval custom is observed only on ceremonial occasions. Draftees have to serve only a twelve-month stint of service. Overtime pay is given for such disagreeable assignments as guard duty and KP.

Socialist Minister of Defense Vredeling (whose name loosely translated means "peacenik") is in charge of the army. He claims to know nothing about the army. It seems he was promised a more prestigious cabinet post, and was given the job in the Defense Department as a sort of consolation prize. "And I have an allergy to uniforms," he protested.

Early America

WAR FOR RENT?

A war with Great Britain seemed imminent so James Madison came up with a unique idea for our national defense. Instead of the United States building a navy from scratch, Madison proposed that the U.S. simply rent Portugal's navy.

* * *

NO SHOTS WERE FIRED AT BUNKER HILL

The first major engagement of the Revolutionary War on June 17, 1775, was not at Bunker Hill.

William Prescott pitted sixteen hundred American irregulars against twenty-five hundred British. The Americans were victorious, killing nearly half the redcoats. Prescott had been ordered to defend Bunker Hill but fortified nearby Breed's Hill instead.

Why "Bunker Hill" was put into military reports is unknown, but speculation has it that Prescott's superiors had already put "Bunker Hill" into their reports by the time the battle was joined and never bothered to correct it.

* * *

CAPTAIN MOLLY

Captain Molly, who's real name was Margaret Cochran Corbin, substituted for her fatally injured husband at the Battle of Fort Washington, N.Y., on November 16, 1776. Under attack, the 2,800 soldiers of the garrison found they were no match for the British, Scottish, and German regulars, who outnumbered them by almost three to one. When British shellfire thundered down on the redoubts, gunners began to fall. Molly Corbin took the place of one of them and wielded a rammer shaft. Her husband dropped mortally wounded, yet Molly kept on serving her gun until she, too, toppled, an arm nearly severed and her breast mangled by grapeshot.

After the capture of the fort, she was taken as a prisoner of war to a Philadelphia hospital where she recovered and was released. Congress voted her a pension of half a soldier's pay for life in 1779. Called "Captain Molly," she wore an artillery coat and accepted the pension as her right; she also insisted on a rum ration due her. She is buried in the cemetery at West Point.

* * *

WHERE ARE THE VOLUNTEERS?

Only 16 percent of the able-bodied males in the American colonies participated in the Revolutionary War.

* * *

SPECIAL SOLDIERS

During the American Revolution, Congress raised eight companies of soldiers—each numbering 120 men—made up entirely of cripples, invalids, blind men and men missing arms or legs.

* * *

THE GIRL WHO OUTRODE PAUL REVERE

During the Revolutionary War, a sixteen-year-old girl went on a ride just as important and perilous as Paul Revere's. The Boston silversmith is a legend, while Sybil Ludington is practically unknown. Few persons outside of Putnam County, in New York, know of her.

Sybil was the daughter of Colonel Henry Ludington, commander of a volunteer regiment in his home village of Fredericksburg, now called Ludingtonville. His regiment guarded all of present Putnam County.

On the evening of April 25, 1777, a force of 2,000 redcoats landed at Westport, Connecticut, and marched inland. They raided Danbury, burned private homes, and wrecked medical supplies and provisions stored there for the Continental Army.

Messengers sped out from Danbury in all directions to get help. One pounded on the door of Colonel Ludington's house just before bedtime. The Colonel's regiment of 421 officers and men were on furlough.

"Can you muster 'em, colonel?" The dusty messenger pleaded. "Danbury's crackling like a campfire. No telling where the redcoats are headed next."

Colonel Ludington had no troops or neighbors nearby to call on. He himself couldn't leave because he had to stay and muster the men as they came in. Finally he went upstairs, where his sixteen-year-old daughter was putting her brothers and sisters to bed. He told her there was a risky job to be done and asked if she could do it. Sybil agreed and got ready to ride off into the night on the family's saddle horse.

The night ride was hazardous for even an armed man. The region was one of several hundred square miles of isolated farms and tiny settlements. Bushwhackers and outlaws, many of them army deserters, lay in wait to molest and rob travelers on the dense trails.

Sybil banged on one door after another, often shouting at the windows: "There's trouble. Bring your gun. The British are burning Danbury. The Colonel wants you right away."

When she got home at daybreak, Sybil saw that practically the whole regiment had assembled in the drill field across from the Ludingtons' house. In a few hours Colonel Ludington's volunteers joined other forces, and, although heavily outnumbered, jolted the British at Ridgefield, Connecticut.

The only monument to Sybil is a modest headstone in the old cemetery of Revolutionary Presbyterians and Episcopalians, near Patterson, New York. The stone merely states Sybil's name, year of birth and death. Like many heroines of America's wars, Sybils contribution remains known only to a few.

*   *   *

BETSY'S FLAG?

No one knows who designed the first American flag.

The Stars and Stripes, first displayed on June 14, 1777, is believed by some to have been an early military banner carried into battle during the American Revolution. The notion that it was designed by Betsy Ross has no historical basis.

* * *

THE SOLDIER WORE SKIRTS

Deborah Sampson Gennett fooled the 4th Massachusetts Regiment, masquerading as a male soldier. She bound her bosom, dressed as a man, and enlisted in 1778.

She fought in skirmishes with the Tories and was twice wounded, a saber slash in a foot and a bullet in one thigh. When wounded in the thigh, she was taken to a hospital. To maintain her disguise, she refused treatment by a surgeon. Sneaking from the hospital at night, she hid in a nearby cave. There she dug a ball shot out of her leg. After a short time, she limped back to her post.

Her "secret" came out at Philadelphia when she fell ill with fever. The attending physician kept her secret, and Gennett was honorably discharged October 23, 1783, as Robert Shurtleff, her assumed name.

* * *

DRESS RIGHT—DRESS!

Soldiers during the American Revolution in General John Burgoyne's regiment were not flogged or imprisoned when they misbehaved. They were made to wear their coats inside-out. Although such punishment seems very minor, Burgoyne's men had so much respect for him that his troops had the lowest disobedience record of any soldiers in the war.

* * *

NEEDED: A FEW GOOD BRITISH MARINES

The Marine Corps was originally a branch of the British army in the American colonies. In 1740 the corps was organized in New York and incorporated into the United States military after the revolution.

* * *

THE INFAMOUS LIFE OF MR. JONES

John Paul Jones, famous naval hero of the American Revolution, led an infamous life. Jones was born to an unmarried woman, was an actor by trade, lived under an assumed name most of his life, was wanted for two murders, practiced piracy, was tried for the rape of a young girl, and died penniless. Born out of wedlock in Scotland and originally named John Paul, he became an actor with a stock company in Jamaica at the age of eleven. He later became a sailor of a West Indies slave ship, where he flogged one shipmate to death and killed another, claiming self-defense, on the island of Tobago. He escaped to America and assumed the name Jones to avoid detection, and eventually distinguished himself during the American Revolution.

After the war Jones became a mercenary sailor, at various times consorting with pirates and selling slaves. Later, he was accused in St. Petersburg, while sailing under the Russian flag, of assaulting a young girl. After a lengthy trial he was acquitted.

The latter part of Jones's life was lived in embittered anonymity. He died in France, a forgotten man, and was buried in an unmarked grave in St. Louis Cemetery. Almost a hundred years later, an American Ambassador named Horace Porter saw to it that Jones's remains were exhumed, brought back to the United States, and buried in a tomb at Annapolis—today a national shrine.

* * *

LOSSES

Only eight men were killed in the Battle of Lexington.

* * *

THE RIDE WAS OVER

Four years after his legendary ride, Paul Revere narrowly escaped charges of "unsoldierly behavior tending to cowardice." The general who pressed charges was the grandfather of poet Henry Wadsworth Longfellow, author of the glamorized "Midnight Ride of Paul Revere."

* * *

WHAT PRICE GLORY?

Paul Revere billed the Massachusetts State House 10 pounds 4 shillings to cover his expenses for his ride.

* * *

THE EYES HAVE IT

William Prescott is believed to have said, "Don't fire until you see the whites of their eyes," during the battle of Bunker Hill. He was not the first to have made such a remark. Credited with similar statements are Prince Charles of Prussia in 1745 ("Silent until you see the whites of their eyes") and Frederick the Great in 1757 (". . . no firing till you see the whites of their eyes"). This of course should not take away from Prescott or his American troops, whose bravery while awaiting to fire is a matter of history.

* * *

WHAT'S IN A MIDDLE NAME?

George Washington had no middle name. Washington's four immediate successors in the presidency—John Adams, Thomas Jefferson, James Madison and James Monroe—were likewise without middle names.

* * *

THE MAN WITHOUT A BIRTHPLACE

Andrew Jackson, "Old Hickory," was born on March 15, 1767, in either North Carolina or South Carolina—no one really knows which. Jackson believed he was born on the farm of his uncle, James Crawford, in Waxhaw Settlement, South Carolina. The Crawford house stood on the west side of the road that formed the boundary between North Carolina and South Carolina at the time.

To this day a "feud" continues with both North and South Carolina claiming to be the state of Jackson's birthplace.

* * *

THE VANISHING MILITARY

Congress abolished the United States Army, the Navy, and the Marine Corps immediately after the end of the American Revolution. Congress became the only national governmental organization because the states feared a standing army.

* * *

YANKEE GO HOME

The term "damned yankee" was not coined by Southerners in reference to Northerners. It first arose during the Revolutionary War and was used against northern "Provincials" by "Yorkers" who were members of General Schuyler's northern army.

* * *

GEORGE'S MOM WANTED HIM AT HOME

Mary Bell Washington did not attend her son's presidential inauguration.

George provided for his mother's financial needs at great personal sacrifice, since he had large holdings but was cash poor. Yet she complained to members of the Virginia legislature that she was in desperate need of funds and solicited their financial aid. When George heard what she had done he begged her to stop. "I am viewed as a delinquent," he wrote to her, "and am considered perhaps by the world as an unjust and undutiful son."

The fact is that she did not seem to really approve of her son George. She was quite angry about his activities during the Revolutionary War. She felt he had no right to go off and play general when she needed him at home to take care of her.

* * *

WE DON'T ALLOW NO CUSSIN' HERE

A General order issued August 3, 1776, by General George Washington from his headquarters at New York stated:

"The General is sorry to be informed that the foolish and wicked practice of profane cursing and swearing, a vice heretofore little known in an American army, is growing into fashion. He hopes the officers will, by example as well as influence, endeavor to check it, and that both they and the men will reflect, that we can little hope of the blessing of Heaven on our arms, if we insult it by our impiety and folly. Added to this, it is a vice so mean and low, without any temptation, that every man of sense and character detests and despises it."

* * *

BLOODY YANKEES!

George Washington created The Order of the Purple Heart in 1782 to commemorate wounds received in battle. But it was awarded just three times in the next 150 years—each time to a man from Connecticut.

* * *

STOP THE WAR

The British orders interfering with U.S. commerce that led to the War of 1812 were actually repealed by Great Britain the day before war was declared by the United States. Rapid communications methods such as the telegraph were not yet invented, so the U.S. had no way of knowing and proceeded with the war as planned.

*　*　*

TREATY? WHAT TREATY?

The famous Battle of New Orleans, won by Andrew Jackson and his troops over the British during the War of 1812, was fought on January 8, 1815—15 days after the war had ended. The news that a treaty ending the conflict had been signed in Europe failed to reach either Jackson or the British troops before the battle. Just as amazing is the fact that Jackson's superiors in Washington were unaware of both the battle and the treaty!

*　*　*

THE BEST SHOOTER WAS A SHAPELY SAILOR

Lucy Brewer was seduced at 17 by a neighbor. Running away to Boston, she was decoyed into a brothel. A privateersman helped her escape the brothel by giving her a set of sailor's clothes. She signed on under Captain Issac Hull, as a marine on the *Constitution*. Proving to be a crack musketeer, she was stationed in a foretop as one of a crew of seven, with male marines loading for her.

When "Old Ironsides" engaged in her historic fight with the British *Guerriere* in the War of 1812, Lucy steadfastly held her position and blazed away from her lofty perch. Bullets cut down the British captain, a mate, the sailing master and many gunners.

On her next cruise, Lucy took part in the fight with the *Java*. Lucy fell from the shrouds into the sea, just before the *Java* struck her colors. She later managed to prevent her comrades from stripping off her wet uniform and discovering her disguise. After three years aboard the *Constitution*, Lucy was granted an honorable discharge. She went home, donned a dress and married. She wrote three books about her experiences.

* * *

WHAT'S IN A NAME?

The term "Uncle Sam" originated from a butcher. During the War of 1812, a meat packer from Troy, New York, Samuel Wilson, supplied the American army with barrels of pork. He stamped the barrels with "EA-US." A group of visitors toured Wilson's plant that same year and asked what the letters stood for. A workman jokingly replied that the US stood for "Uncle Sam" (an eyewitness account of the conversation was reported in the *New York Gazette* and *General Advertiser* on May 12, 1820) and the name caught on. The character of Uncle Sam was appearing in numerous political cartoons by the next decade.

* * *

JINXED SHIP

Owing to the misadventures of the first American naval vessel to be called the *Chesapeake*, the U.S. Navy has never given this name to another combatant ship. In 1807, the captain of this frigate, unprepared to fight, struck his flag and allowed his vessel to be searched after being fired upon by the *H.M.S. Leopard*. Again in 1813, the crew of the *Chesapeake*, unwilling to continue a battle, surrendered and the ship was captured by the *H.M.S. Shannon*.

* * *

THE FIRST PRESIDENT TO FACE ENEMY GUNFIRE WHILE IN OFFICE

President James Madison was the first president to face enemy gunfire while in office and the first and only president to exercise actively his authority as Commander-in-Chief.

On August 19, 1814, General Robert Ross, in command of British regulars, and Admiral George Cockburn, commanding the Marines, landed at Benedict, Md., on the Patuxent River. They started a forty-mile march to Washington, D.C. Five days later, at Bladensburg, Md., they encountered and routed the militia and marines under General William Henry Winder, who fled to Georgetown after a losing battle. President James Madison, on August 25, assumed command of Commodore Joshua Barney's battery, known as "Blarney's Battery," stationed a half-mile north of Bladensburg, Md., to forestall the capture of Washington by the British.

* * *

THE PROUD—THE FEW

A familiar slogan of the U.S. Marines is, "The proud, the few, the Marines." Yet the term marine began use as a derogatory reference.

In the early 1820's, marines were thought of as models of gullibility by sailors. The general consensus was that even though marines might not want to put up with nonsense, their natural foolishness would lead them to do so anyway.

In 1840 one popular meaning of marine was "an ignorant or clumsy seaman"; another, from 1800, was "an empty bottle."

* * *

POE BARES IT ALL

Edgar Allen Poe was expelled from West Point in 1831 for "gross neglect of duty" because he appeared at a public parade naked. Poe took literally the parade dress instructions for "white belts and gloves, under arms." Appearing on the parade ground, rifle balanced on his bare shoulder, Poe made his appearance wearing nothing but a smile, white belt and gloves.

* * *

WHO WILL CARRY THE FLAG?

It was forbidden for any soldier or military unit of the U.S. Army to carry a flag into battle until 1834. In 1834 the privilege was awarded to American artillery units only. It was not until late in 1876 that the Marine Corps could carry the flag; the cavalry in 1887. Only regimental colors were taken to war before these dates.

* * *

WHO INVENTED THE BOWIE KNIFE?

The bowie knife, credited to and associated with the famous defender of the Alamo, James Bowie, was actually invented by his lesser-known brother, Rezin Pleasant Bowie. James became identified with the famous knife because he carried it everywhere and was adept at using it.

* * *

SHORT WAR

In 1871 a month-long war ensued when Korea refused to do business with the U.S. The war ended in a draw. American ships sailed off claiming victory. The Koreans declared they had driven the Americans away.

* * *

THE HOME WHERE THE CIVIL WAR BEGAN AND ENDED

The first major battle of the Civil War took place at Bull Run Creek, near the home of Wilmer McLean. McLean feared for his family's safety, so to get away from the combat zone, he moved his family from Bull Run to a remote village named Appomattox Court House. Generals Lee and Grant met for the signing of surrender papers in the parlor of McLean's house in

Appomattox. Ironically, the Civil War had started near McLean's home at Bull Run, and ended in his home.

* * *

MAKE WAR, NOT WAR

On April 12, 1861, shortly before the Civil War began, Secretary of State William H. Seward came up with a clever plan to avert the impending catastrophe. Seward presented his plan to President Lincoln: provoke a war with a foreign power.

Seward wrote a memo on April 1 to Lincoln titled "Some Thoughts for the President's Consideration." His advice was that the U.S. should demand "explanations" from France and Spain for their intervention in the Caribbean: The U.S. would declare war on the countries if they did not respond. Lincoln turned down the proposal.

Seward devised the plan thinking war would unite the states. He felt if Spain could be provoked to fight, the South would quickly join forces with the North, eager to claim the Spanish colonies of Puerto Rico and Cuba as slave territories. The U.S. might obtain some island bases in any case.

* * *

FIRING AT FORT SUMTER

General P.G.T. Beauregard was in charge of the Confederate troops surrounding Fort Sumter on April 1861. Major Robert Anderson, who had once been Beauregard's artillery instructor at West Point, was the leader of the Union garrison inside the fort.

The siege of Fort Sumter lasted a day and a half, and miraculously no one was killed. Major Anderson and his men surrendered, and were permitted to leave the harbor on Union supply ships. They fired a cannon in a salute to the Stars and Stripes as a final tribute to the Union. The gun exploded and killed a Union soldier—the only casualty of the first engagement of the Civil War.

*   *   *

AND THEN THERE WERE ELEVEN

The Confederacy officially included only 7 states, when the firing on Ft. Sumter began. South Carolina had been the first to secede, in December, 1860, and six other states seceded before the war began in April of 1861. Shortly thereafter, Virginia, Arkansas, North Carolina, and Tennessee joined the Confederacy.

*   *   *

THE GREAT CAMEL CAPER

In 1853 Secretary of War Jefferson Davis, recommended that the United States buy a tract of land from Mexico south of the Gila river to provide a route to California that skirted the Rocky Mountains.

The difficulties of supplying the isolated frontier posts in the arid regions of the Southwest prompted an interesting experiment in the use of camels. Davis thought that the camel, which for centuries had been used as a pack and riding animal in the deserts of Africa and Asia, might solve the Army's supply problem. He obtained a small appropriation from Congress in 1856 and had 30 camels purchased and shipped to Texas. The animals easily adapted to the rough terrain and were able to carry twice as much as a horse could pull in a wagon, and to walk surefootedly over ground no wagon could cross. The next Secretary of War, John B. Floyd, was so enthusiastic about the idea that he asked Congress for money to buy a thousand camels. But Congress refused to appropriate the funds. Nevertheless, the original group of camels and their descendants carried supplies in the Southwest until the Civil War, and some were even reported to have carried the Confederate mails in Texas.

The Civil War ended the U.S. Army's camel experiment, and the construction of the transcontinental railways after the war made further use of the camels unnecessary.

* * *

THE CHIRPING GENERAL

General Richard S. Ewell, who fought bravely for the Confederacy at Winchester and Gettysburg, at times hallucinated that he was a bird. For hours at a stretch, he would sit in his tent softly chirping to himself. At meal times he would accept nothing except a few grains of wheat or sunflower seeds.

* * *

WHERE WAS THE BATTLE OF SHILOH FOUGHT?

One of the bloodiest battles ever fought in North America occurred on April 6 and 7, 1862, at the so-called Battle of Shiloh.

Union forces, led by General Grant, lost over thirteen thousand men, and Confederate forces, led by General Albert Johnson, sustained losses of over eleven thousand.

The bloody battle was not fought at Shiloh, but Pittsburg Landing, Tennessee. The battle became known as Shiloh because of the presence of Shiloh church located near the center of the battlefield. The church's name originated from a region known as Shiloh, a Bibical site north of Jerusalem which was destroyed around 1000 B.C. by the Philestines.

* * *

THE DEATH OF "STONEWALL"

General Thomas J. "Stonewall" Jackson and his brigade was the Confederacy's most devastating war machine.

Jackson's First Brigade was trained to precision. The discipline, the unflinching obedience of Jackson's men, the military brilliance of their leader combined to comprise a virtually unconquerable instrument of war.

Jackson's last battle took place in May 1863 in an encounter with Union general Joseph Hooker near Chancellorsville, Virginia. After already having divided his troops, Jackson divided them again, swung around to the right in a surprise attack and extended himself and his division beyond his own lines. They routed the enemy.

The battle had been won but General "Stonewall" Jackson, returning from the attack, was shot three times.

Considering the morale of his men to the last, he

had requested that his wounds be kept secret. But his men knew all along. Among the strict orders Jackson had issued to the brigade before the battle was to immediately gun down any unknown soldiers, and to ask questions later.

That is why Jackson's men, ever obedient, responded to the rustling in the thick woods of Chancellorsville by opening fire upon an "unknown soldier" returning from battle beyond his own lines. The "unknown soldier" was General Jackson.

Jackson's wounds in themselves were not fatal. He lived for several days in a weakened condition—and then died of pneumonia.

* * *

BURNSIDE'S BLUNDERS

Civil War general Ambrose Burnside could attest to the wisdom of "Murphy's Law": "Whatever can go wrong will."

On Ambrose's wedding day his wife-to-be took one last look at him and responded with an emphatic "No!" when the minister asked her if she took this man to be her lawful wedded husband.

From the moment he entered the military, Burnside began to be a luckless soldier. He graduated low in his class at West Point and excelled more in extracurricular singing and cooking than in military tactics. After a tour with the cavalry in the West, he resigned from the Army in 1853, to set up the Bristol Rifle Works in Rhode Island, where he manufactured the breech-loading Burnside carbine that he invented. He had no luck with the business and it failed. He reentered the

Army at the outbreak of the Civil War.

Burnside's expedition to the North Carolina coast in 1862 resulted in the capture of Roanoke Island, New Bern, Beaufort, and Fort Major. He was soon promoted to major general. Yet when he later took command of the Army of the Potomac his plan to capture Fredericksburg resulted in a slaughter so bloody that a special truce had to be called to bury the 100,000 Union dead—making Fredericksburg long known as Burnside's Slaughter Pen.

In 1864 Burnside approved a plan to dig a tunnel under the Confederate lines, fill it with high explosives and attack the moment the charges were set off. The tunnel was built, the attack was made, and the attack repulsed. General Burnside was relieved of his command by a court of inquiry and was nearly put out of the Army.

For all of his mistakes Burnside's winning personality and patriotic spirit gave him political success. He was elected governor of Rhode Island for three terms, and U.S. senator for two terms, from 1875 until his death in 1881, aged 57.

Burnside was innovative in one special way, starting a style that remains popular today. As a general in the field he chose to wear the hair on his face in a new way, shaving his chin smooth below a full moustache and sidebar whiskers. Thousands imitated him and his burnsides, because they were only on the sides of his face, were soon called sideburns.

*   *   *

RESPECT

During the Civil War undertakers were addressed as "Doctor."

* * *

THE SOUTHERN WOMAN WHO HELPED LINCOLN SAVE THE UNION

On November, 1861, the U.S. stood on the brink of dissolution. A petite Southern Woman, Anna Ella Carrol, devised a brilliant military plan that saved it.

Anne, as she was called, was born on August 29, 1815, and grew up on a 2,000-acre tobacco plantation in Somerset County, Md.

Anne was taught at home and perfected her reading by studying her father's entire collection of law books.

Fifteen-year-old Anne soon entered into political circles, where she was to render incalculable service as adviser to politicians and presidents when her father was elected governor of Maryland.

President Lincoln had been close friends with Anne for years and he turned to her for advice during the difficult summer of 1861. Helping to fill in for Lincoln's lack of military expertise, Anne became his unofficial cabinet member.

Lincoln recommended that Anne be put in the War Department's employ to write for the government and to scout out the dire military situation in the West. Few of the enlisted men Anne interviewed and none of the officers, including Generals Sherman and Grant, thought the Union could be saved.

Union preparations for a gunboat assault on the Mississippi fortresses were an obvious necessity. Although the Confederates were ready to meet the attack, Anne surmised correctly that the southern troops had lowered their guard at Fort Henry on the Tennessee river. She quickly set about gathering military information. Anne came up with a plan and had it sent to President Lincoln.

The plan was put into action and, as Anne had predicted, Fort Henry fell to Major General Halleck, who was hailed as a hero. Lincoln ordered follow-up attacks on railway connections, that resulted in victory after victory for the Union. But the Union's success was not credited to Anne Carrol. Army generals tried to take the credit that rightfully belonged to Anne and President Lincoln implored Anne, saying, "Could I dare let it be known that the armies of the U.S. are moving under the directing hand of a woman?"

Anne was not named by Congress as the hero, but Representative Roscoe Conkling went on record as saying the credit should not be appropriated by those to whom it was not due, nor denied to those who deserved it. Later it was entered in the *Congressional Record* that the movement of troops to the Memphis and Charleston Railroad had been Anne's idea and had proceeded according to her detailed instructions.

Stanton—appointed to carry out her overall plan—concurred, saying, "She . . . did the great work, that made the others famous."

* * *

MARY E. WALKER: MEDAL OF HONOR WINNER

One woman in American history was awarded the

nation's highest award for valor, the Medal of Honor. Doctor Mary Edwards Walker served in the Union Army during the Civil War. She became the first woman officer in the United States Army, and the first female military surgeon.

She was captured at Chattanooga and taken to Libby prison, an infamous Confederate camp in Richmond. As shown by Army record, Dr. Walker became the only woman prisoner who was eventually exchanged for a man of similar rank. The Judge Advocate General noted that while in Chattanooga "she frequently passed beyond our lines far within those of the enemy, and at one time gained information that led Gen. Sherman so to modify his strategic operations as to save himself from a serious reverse and obtain success where defeat before seemed inevitable."

Major Generals George H. Thomas and William T. Sherman recommended Dr. Walker for the Medal of Honor. On November 11, 1865, President Andrew Johnson signed the executive order awarding the Medal of Honor and two other awards to Dr. Walker for her work "as the first woman physician to serve in the Army without concealing her sex."

The Medal of Honor awarded Dr. Walker was, by adverse action of the Board of Medals Awards, striken from the list February 15, 1917. This action was taken on the grounds that "nothing (had) been found in the records to show the specific Act or Acts for which the decoration was originally awarded." Dr. Walker refused to relinquish her Medal of Honor and wore it for the rest of her life.

In 1977, the Army Board for Correction of Military Records concluded that "when consideration is given to her total contribution, her acts of distinguished gallantry, self-sacrifice, patriotism, dedication and unflinching loyalty to her country, despite the apparent discrimination because of her sex, the award of the Medal of Honor appears to have been appropriate, and that the award was in consonance with the criteria established by the Act of April 27, 1917, and in keeping with the highest traditions of military service.

* * *

THE SECRET LIFE OF FRANKLIN THOMPSON

Franklin Thompson, 2nd Michigan Volunteer Infantry, Company F, a nurse and spy in McClellan's Army, was born Sarah Emma Edmonds.

In April, 1863, Emma suffered again from the severe malarial fever that she had contracted originally in the Chickahominy swamps. She applied for furlough, but her papers came back marked "Disapproved." She was afraid to go to the hospital, as her sex would have been discovered. She therefore went AWOL and was listed as a deserter from the 2nd Michigan as of April 22, 1863.

After resting for a few weeks, Emma began to write her memoirs, *Nurse And Spy Or Unsexed, The Female Soldier*. When fully recovered from her illness she returned to the Army, "In another costume." As a woman she served with the Christian Commission at Harper's Ferry, Va., until the close of the war.

Sarah married Linus Seelye in 1867, and later moved to Kansas. There she wrote to some of her former comrades of the 2nd Michigan Infantry. A few of her comrades of the "Old Second" induced "Frank

Thompson" to attend a reunion of the regiment.

After 20 years, everyone had changed, but the veterans were more than mildly shocked to discover that Franklin Thompson was now Mrs. Linus Seelye! After the initial shock, Emma's old comrades gave her a royal reception.

A short while later active steps were taken by the regimental association and a committee was appointed to restore her to honorable standing on the records of the War Department, to grant her an honorable discharge, a pension, back pay and bounty. The 48th Congress passed an act removing Emma's status as a deserter and granting her a pension of twelve dollars a month.

On September 5, 1898, Emma Edmonds Seelye died and was buried near La Porte, Texas. On Memorial Day in 1901, Emma Seelye was removed to Washington Cemetery in Houston. She was re-entered in the G.A.R. burial plot in a grave indicated by a simple metal marker, and is said to be the only woman buried there.

* * *

BRIDGET DIVERS: HELL-FOR-LEATHER CAVALRY WOMAN

When the bugles sounded, "Michigan Bridget," as all General Philip Sheridan's horsemen came to call her, followed her husband off to the Civil War in the 1st Michigan Cavalry.

Bridget Divers became a hell-for-leather cavalry woman. She went through eight to ten horses—several being shot from under her—in four years of hard campaigning. In action she turned Irish, and if a trooper fell, she never hesitated to take his place in a charge.

In the Battle of Cedar Creek, she found herself at one time cut off and surrounded by the enemy, but managed by an adroit movement to escape capture. She rode for four nights without sleep during one of General Sheridan's raids, then took part in a cavalry engagement in which her colonel was wounded and her captain killed.

Not even with the close of the war did her self-imposed duties end. She became attached to the free and spirited life of the cavalry soldier and became a member of the detachment that crossed the great plains and the Rocky Mountains for Indian service on the western frontier.

*   *   *

SHE FOUGHT BY HIS SIDE IN THE WAR

A Wisconsin girl followed her soldier-lover through four years of active service in the Civil War. Ellen Goodridge left home and followed her lover to Washington in 1861.

Ellen and her lover, James Hendrick, were in every great battle that was fought in Virginia, and in the intervals Ellen often went with him on skirmishes and raids. On one such occasion she received a painful wound in her arm from a minie ball.

*   *   *

THE BEARDED LADY SOLDIER

Loretta Velasquez, a Cuban, joined the Confederate

forces with her adventurer husband. After her husband's enlistment and early death, she raised a company of cavalry in Arkansas and equipped it at her own expense. She took a man's name, wore a false beard and mustache and avoided bathing with men.

Disguised as a man, Loretta went to Virginia and took part in First Manassas, and served for several months under Colonel Dreaux before her sex was discovered. She was ordered home, but resumed her disguise and went to Columbus, Ky., and fought under General Polk in Kentucky and Tennessee were she was wounded twice.

Later Loretta was engaged by the Confederacy as a spy and special agent. As a counterspy in Washington, she managed to become a member of the operating staff of Colonel Lafayette C. Baker, Chief of the U.S. Secret Service.

Loretta survived the war to write her adventurous autobiography many years later.

* * *

YOUNGEST BRIGADIER GENERAL

Galusha Pennypacker was too young to vote when he became a major general. He was 16 years old when he joined the U.S. Army in 1861, and became a quartermaster-sergeant with the 9th Pennsylvania Volunteers. He was promoted to captain that August in the 97th Pennsylvania Volunteers. His men greatly admired him, and the boy-soldier was a colonel by 1864. At age 20, he was wounded at Green Plains, Va., but soon recovered and went back into action.

On January 15, 1865, at Fort Fisher, N.C.,

Pennypacker led a brigade across enemy lines, planted a regimental flag and was badly wounded. A month later, he was promoted to brigadier general, making him the youngest soldier to achieve that rank on either side in the war. In March, not yet 21, he was commissioned a major general.

* * *

MANY FLAGS OF THE CONFEDERACY

The Confederate States of America had more than one flag during the Civil War. The familiar "Rebel Flag" was one of four flags used. The first flag was raised in March, 1861, and consisted of one horizontal white bar between two red bars, with a field of seven white stars. But in July of that year, during the Battle of Manassas, the Confederate forces had difficulty distinguishing their flag from that of the Union forces. A new flag, the "Battle Flag," was raised shortly thereafter. This was the familiar flag, with a red field crossed diagonally by blue bars with 13 white stars.

A third flag was raised in 1863, a plain white flag with the "Battle Flag" in the upper left corner. But many felt that when this flag hung limp it looked like a white flag of truce. So a fourth Confederate flag was raised; this flag was identical to the third except for a red bar down the right edge.

* * *

ROBERT E. LEE AND HIRAM GRANT

General Robert E. Lee surrendered to General Hiram Grant, thus ending the Civil War. Ridiculous you say?

Everyone knows the Union general's name was Ulysses S. Grant. U.S. were not Grant's original initials; nor were "Ulysses" and "Simpson" his given names. Grant was born Hiram Ulysses Grant. He was given the patriotic initials U.S. by a congressman who sponsored him for the West Point Military Academy. The congressman dropped the Hiram, retained the Ulysses, and added the boy's mother's maiden name of Simpson when reporting Grant's name to the registrar.

The story that General Lee turned over his sword to General Grant after the surrender, and that Grant immediately returned the sword to Lee, is without foundation. Grant had specified that all rebel officers be allowed to keep their swords and denied that such an occurrence had ever taken place.

Lee was the son of George Washington's cavalry leader and married Martha Washington's great-granddaughter.

On April 18, 1861, Lee was called to Washington and offered command of a new army being formed to force the seceded states back into the Union, by President Lincoln. Lee, while he opposed secession, also opposed war, and "Could take no part in an invasion of the Southern States." Meanwhile, President Lincoln called on Virginia to furnish troops for the invasion. A Virginia convention, which had previously voted 2 to 1 against secession, now voted 2 to 1 against furnishing troops for an invasion and to secede, and Lee resigned from the army in which he had served for 36 years to offer his services to the "defense of (his) native state."

Lee and Grant were not without their idiosyncrasies; for instance, during the Civil War, Grant would often eat a cucumber soaked in vinegar for breakfast. If he ate meat at all, it had to be cooked black: he detested the sight of rare meat because the blood made him feel queasy.

Lee had a pet hen which laid an egg under his cot each day, at the height of the war. He never forgot to leave the tent flap open for her. Lee saw to it that the hen traveled with the army, even on so fateful a campaign as the invasion which ended at Gettysburg. When he began to retreat from that field, the hen was nowhere to be found. Lee joined the search for his pet, and was not content until she was discovered safely perched in his wagon.

Grant died July 23, 1885, at Mount McGregor. He was buried in Riverside Park, New York City, where an elaborate tomb was dedicated in 1897.

Lee died October 12, 1870, just after a flood had swept the hill country. C.M. Koones, the Lexington undertaker, was embarrassed to report that he had no coffins, since the three he had recently imported from Richmond had been swept away from his river wharf.

Two young men volunteered to search for a coffin for the Lee funeral. They searched for hours before discovering one that had been swept over a dam and had lodged on an island two miles downstream. This became the coffin in which the Confederacy's greatest figure was buried. The casket was too short for Lee and he was buried without his shoes. (Lee was a small man; his shoe size was four and a half.)

*   *   *

DAMN THE TORPEDOES

"Damn the torpedoes—full speed ahead!" This remark attributed to Admiral David Glasgow Farragut at the Battle of Mobile Bay on August 5, 1864, has no significance when applied to torpedoes as we know them today. The first self-propelled torpedo was not perfected until after the Civil War. Before that, torpedo was a name used for what we call mines today. Admiral Farragut's torpedoes were actually beer kegs filled with powder.

* * *

"BRAINS OF THE CONFEDERACY" NEVER BECAME A CITIZEN

Judah Philip Benjamin, noted lawyer, United States Senator, Attorney General, Secretary of War and Secretary of State in the Confederate cabinet of Jefferson Davis, never technically became a citizen of the United States or the Confederate States of America.

Benjamin, known as "the brains of the Confederacy," was born a British subject. His parents (Philip Benjamin, an English Jew, and Rebecca de Mendes, a Portuguese Jew) attempted to emigrate to New Orleans in 1811, but after learning that the British were blockading the mouth of the Mississippi, lived a few years on the island of St. Croix in the British West Indies, where Judah was born. When Judah was four years old in 1815, the family moved to the United States and settled in Wilmington, North Carolina. There is no evidence that either Benjamin or his father ever became American citizens.

* * *

JOE'S HOOKERS

"Fighting Joe" Hooker, a Union Army general in the Civil War, enjoyed spending his free time with paid companions.

He frequented so many of New Orleans' prostitutes that the girls came to be called "Hooker's Division." Some etymologists hold that this was the origin of the word "hooker" as a slang term for prostitute.

* * *

HOLDOUTS

Four slave states did not join the Confederacy during the American Civil War. Delaware, Kentucky, Maryland, and Missouri remained nominally a part of the Union.

* * *

WAR IS HELL

General William Tecumseh Sherman is attributed with saying, "War is hell." Sherman could not remember ever having uttered the phrase. Some authorities think it comes from a speech Sherman made to a GAR convention at Columbus, Ohio, on August 11, 1880: "There is many a boy here today who looks on war as all glory, but, boys, it is all hell."

* * *

TO BE OR NOT TO BE A BANK TELLER?

William Tecumseh Sherman began his career in banking and law, after a disciplinary problem at West Point. Bored with military life in Florida and California, he resigned his commission September 6, 1853.

Later, after law and banking proved unsuccessful for him, he was appointed a colonel in the U.S. Army in May 1861, at the start of the Civil War, and became a general after the first Battle of Bull Run.

* * *

THE SHRINKING CONFEDERATE DOLLAR

The money issued by the Confederate States of America during the Civil War at first commanded a slight premium. But as the war progressed, the value steadily declined until during the last days of the Confederacy it required $800 to $1,000 in Confederate money to buy a one-dollar greenback.

The following table shows the declining value of the Confederate dollar during the progression of the war.

June 1, 1861	90 Cents
Dec 1, 1861	80 Cents
Dec 15, 1861	75 Cents
Feb 1, 1862	60 Cents
Feb 1, 1863	20 Cents
Jun 1, 1863	8 Cents
Jan 1, 1864	2 Cents
Nov 1, 1864	4½ Cents
Jan 1, 1865	2½ Cents
Apr 1, 1865	1½ Cents

* * *

PLAY DIXIE FOR ME

The afternoon that Abraham Lincoln learned of Lee's surrender, he ordered the band to play "Dixie" on the front lawn of the White House.

"I have always thought 'Dixie' one of the best tunes I have ever heard," he said. "Our adversaries over the way attempted to appropriate it, but I insisted yesterday that we fairly captured it. I presented the opinion to the Attorney General, and he gave it as his legal opinion that it is, our lawful prize. I now request the band to favor me with its performance."

The band immediately struck up the melody that had been the anthem and battle cry of the former enemy.

* * *

OLDEST SOLDIER

The oldest age to which a veteran soldier has lived is 113 years, one day. John B. Salling of the Army of the Confederate States of America was the last accepted survivor of the U.S. Civil War. He died March 16, 1959, in Kingsport, Tennessee.

* * *

LAST CASUALTIES OF THE CIVIL WAR

The last soldiers killed in the Civil War, died on May 22, 1865. Three Confederate soldiers refused to accept Lee's surrender. A Virginian named Bordunix and two Confederate comrades set out to attack 500 Federal troopers at the courthouse in Floyd, Va. The Federals were taken completely by surprise when the three Confederates began firing at them. Two Union soldiers fell wounded. The Federal troops gave chase and cornered the Confederates in a graveyard six miles away. The Federals wanted to take the three rebels alive, but angry spectators urged the Federals to fight to the death. The Federal troops fired one synchronized round of over 300 shots. The last three confederates were killed, and buried where they fell.

* * *

A U.S. STATE JUST FOR INDIANS

American Indians were so important to the Confederacy during the Civil War that they were promised their own state if the South won.

An Arkansas lawyer named Albert Pike was sent to Indian Territory in 1861 to try to persuade the Cherokees, Choctaws, Chickasaws, Creeks and Seminoles over to the Confederate side. The Indians were guaranteed representation in the Confederate Congress and an all-Indian state, to be established in the area of what is now Oklahoma.

Indians were interested in the deal because many of them were slaveholders with a vivid interest in the Southern cause.

In all about 5,550 Indians fought for the South, 4,000 for the North.

Most of the Indians were courageous soldiers. In fact the last Confederate leader to surrender was a Cherokee Chief, Brigadier General Stand Watie. It wasn't until June 23, 1865—more than two months after Robert E. Lee surrendered at Appomatox—that Waite gave up the fight.

* * *

WHOSE TOWN IS IT ANYWAY?

Winchester, a strategic point in the lower Shenandoah Valley in Virginia, changed hands between the Federals and Confederates 68 times during the Civil War. Time after time, from the beginning to the end of that conflict, the town was taken or occupied by one army only to be lost or abandoned to the other. Later, several important engagements took place in the vicinity of Winchester, and Stonewall Jackson's many operations in the Shenandoah Valley gave it the name of Stonewall's Way.

* * *

PAY AND STAY

Some of our chief executives were war heroes; Grant, Washington, Jackson and Eisenhower were all famous generals.

But all those "called" did not wish to serve. Grover Cleveland, "drafted" into the Union Army during the Civil War, paid a substitute $150 to serve in his place and stayed home to support his mother and sister while his two brothers were off fighting for the Union. Cleveland's actions were completely legal under the terms of the Conscription Act of 1863.

* * *

IT'S NOT THE ENEMY THAT GETS YOU . . .

The Union Army lost more men as a result of disease than it lost in battle during the Civil War. The same was true in the Spanish-American War and World War I. The United States suffered 1,733 battle deaths, and lost 11,550 men to "other causes," during the Mexican War.

* * *

WIDOWS OF CIVIL WAR SOLDIERS STILL RECEIVING PENSIONS

Widows of Civil War veterans are still receiving pension checks from the Veterans Administration.

At this writing, there are 43 Civil War widows, each collecting a monthly benefit of about $70. The 14 Confederate ladies have received benefits since 1958, when Congress forgivingly declared them eligible.

Between 1890, when the pension program was inaugurated, and 1905, when a cutoff was declared on eligibility, many teen-aged girls married aging Union vets to take advantage of the pension. The average age of the 43 surviving widows is 90.

Pensions are still being paid out to widows from the Indian wars, the Spanish-American War, the Boxer Rebellion and the Philippine Insurrection. In some instances, the costs of these benefits has surpassed the cost of the war in which they were earned.

* * *

HANGED FOR MUTINY

Only one U.S. Navy man was ever hanged for mutiny—the son of a Secretary of War. Midshipman Philip Spencer was found guilty, along with two enlisted men, in 1842, of scheming to turn their ship, the U.S.S. *Somers*, to piracy.

* * *

THE DAY THE GENERAL WORE SKIRTS

The American army stationed at Corpus Christi during the Mexican War faced a monotonous winter in 1845–1846.

To help relieve the boredom, the men formed a theatrical group. They staged Shakespeare's *Othello*, and in this all-soldier production the part of Desdemona was played by Ulysses S. Grant.

* * *

SAN PATRICIO'S BRIGADE

So many Americans fought for the enemy during the Mexican War that they formed their own brigade.

In the spring of 1846, as opposition to the U.S. annexation of Texas was growing, morale in the U.S. Army was low because of arbitrary and unduly harsh punishment. As a result, Mexican General Pedro de Ampudia had no problem luring hundreds of U.S. soldiers to his side with promises of generous land grants, quick military promotions and Mexican citizenship.

At the beginning Americans fought as replacements for the Mexicans who were put out of action. Later they became the San Patricio Brigade, which consisted of three artillery companies. The San Patricios fought ruthlessly against their former comrades, inflicting many casualties. The San Patricios were finally defeated at Churubusco in 1847. The captured traitors were court-martialed on charges of treason and desertion. The punishment consisted of hard-labor sentences, head-shaving or having the letter "D" branded on their cheeks. The desertions continued nevertheless, and the San Patricio Brigade was not disbanded until the Mexican War ended in May 1848.

* * *

THE CHOPPER IS BORN

The first fully automatic machine gun came into being in 1884. Herman Maxim made use of the energy of the recoil of a fired bullet to eject the spent cartridge and then load the next.

* * *

THE FIRST KOREAN WAR

Three Americans died and 10 were wounded. There were nearly 350 Korean casualties during the first war between the U.S. and Korea.

In the 1860's, American traders began to consider Korea as a potential source of trade. But the Koreans viewed Westerners as barbarians.

In May 1871, Frederick Low, the U.S. minister to China, went to Korea hoping to break through Korea's isolationist policies. Washington had been alerted a few months earlier that an American-owned merchant ship had been destroyed in Korean waters by suspicious natives. Admiral John Rodgers with a flotilla of five run-down boats, manned by 1,500 sailors and marines, accompanied Low to try to convince Korea of the good intentions of the United States.

Low's diplomatic mission failed. Rodgers led two of his ships up the Han River and the Koreans fired on the ships. The Americans returned the fire, killing several Koreans. The U.S. forces then easily defeated the Koreans.

The undeclared four-day Korean War was not reported by the U.S. press until a month after the fighting was over. The New York *Herald* ran the heading: "Our Little War with the Heathen."

* * *

THANKS, I NEEDED THAT

Frank Harrington was one of 50 men attacked by 500 Cheyenne Indians in 1868 when he was hit in the fore-head by an arrow.

He could not pull it loose, but a glancing rifle shot hit it and knocked it free.

* * *

THE GREATEST, NOT THE SMARTEST

George Armstrong Custer had the dubious honor of finishing last in his graduating class at West Point. In 1861, the future general ranked 35th in his graduating class of 35 students.

* * *

CUSTER'S GHOST RIDERS

In May 1876, General George A. Custer and his 7th Cavalry Regiment, consisting of about 600 men, were assigned to join an expedition against the Sioux Indians in what is now southeastern Montana. Residents saw the command marching out of Fort Abraham Lincoln in a cloud of dust and observed a strange omen of the fate that would befall the regiment. They watched in amazement as almost half the regiment appeared to ride off into the sky and vanish.

A little more than a month later, at the Battle of the Little Big Horn, on June 25, Custer and 264 of his men were outflanked and killed by the forces of the Sioux chiefs Sitting Bull and Crazy Horse. As the vision, or mirage, had indicated, about half his regiment was lost.

* * *

WHAT REALLY HAPPENED AT THE BATTLE OF THE LITTLE BIG HORN?

George Armstrong Custer was not a general at the time of the battle of the Little Big Horn. He had reached the rank of major general during the Civil War, but as with many wartime promotions, this was removed after the war and Custer was demoted to the rank of captain.

In 1866 Custer was made lieutenant colonel and ordered to Kansas to take part in General Winfield S. Hancock's expedition to awe hostile Plains Indians with the military strength of the U.S. Army. Custer disobeyed orders to wait for supplies to be loaded at Ft. Harker, and went to Ft. Riley to visit his wife, Elizabeth. He was court-martialed in 1867 at Ft.

Leavenworth and suspended for one year without pay.

Increased hostility of the Plains Indians led to his reinstatement and in September, 1868, he rejoined the 7th Cavalry in Kansas, as lieutenant colonel.

Custer, in command of two columns of a projected two-pronged attack under the command of General Alfred Terry, arrived near the Little Big Horn on the night of June 24, 1876. Terry's column was to join him in two days. Custer was determined to wipe out Sitting Bull's hidden encampment by himself and decided not to wait for Terry. On the morning of June 25, he divided his men into three battalions. Of the 266 men who followed Custer into battle, not one remained alive. A single horse, Comanche, survived and for many years thereafter appeared in the 7th Cavalry parades, saddled but riderless.

As for the long golden locks that "General" Custer sported in Hollywood movies, here are the words of the Hunkpapa Chief Crow King: "No warrior knew Custer in the fight. We did not know him, dead or alive. When the fight was over, the Chiefs gave orders to look for the long-haired chiefs among the dead, but no chiefs with long hair could be found."

* * *

PRAISE FOR THE HERO

A biography of George Armstrong Custer, by James Warner Bellah, in its entirety reads: "To put it mildly, this was an oddball."

* * *

THE DISAPPEARING LIBERTY BELL

In 1893, the Columbia Liberty Bell disappeared without a trace.

The 13,000-pound, 7-foot-tall bell was specially cast by the Daughters of the American Revolution for the Columbian Exposition in Chicago. The exposition commemorated the 400th anniversary of Columbus's discovery of America. The bell was made of donated metal objects associated with the fight for liberty. Among the objects were the flintlock from Thomas Jefferson's rifle, old coins, thimbles, wedding rings, 250,000 pennies, and two lead bullets that had met in midair to form a U (for Union) during a Civil War battle.

The bell was scheduled to go on tour after the exposition. But it disappeared and was never found again.

* * *

THE ROUGH WALKERS

Teddy Roosevelt's Rough Riders became legendary in the Spanish-American War. The Rough Riders charged up San Juan Hill in Cuba to defeat the Spanish and end the conflict. The Rough Riders walked and ran up the hill and did not ride up as everyone believed. They went up the hill on foot, because they had no horses. The Rough Riders never rode at all in the war, they fought every battle on foot.

Assistant Secretary of the Navy Theodore Roosevelt secured Congressional approval for recruiting a volunteer regiment of cavalry at the outbreak of the war in 1898. Roosevelt selected 1,000 men as his Rough Riders; among the men choosen were Harvard bluebloods, horsemen, cowboys and famous athletes.

After two months of rigorous training in Texas, the Rough Riders were ready for Cuba. But when the regiment embarked on the troopships, there was only enough room on board for 560 men and absolutely no room for their 1,200 horses and pack mules.

Roosevelt's Rough Riders became foot soldiers of the war for two months.

*   *   *

INFANTRY ON TWO WHEELS

The United States occupied Cuba at the end of the Spanish-American War in 1898. Outbreaks of malaria and yellow fever and rioting mobs in the streets created havoc in the country. Lieutenant James Moss was sent with his troops to maintain order, and they were successful. Moss's 25th Infantry consisted of only 100 men and was unique in several ways. The Infantry was a bicycle corps—they all rode bicycles, they were all black, and they never once used their weapons while in Cuba.

*   *   *

REMEMBER THE *MAINE*

The *Maine* was the United States battleship that was damaged so severely that the Spanish-American was begun because of it. When the news broke out that a Spanish mine had sunk our ship in Havana Harbor, the now famous war cry was born: "Remember the *Maine!*"

At 9:40 p.m. on February 15, 1898, the American battleship *Maine* exploded in the harbor of Havana,

Cuba. There were 354 officers and men aboard; 266 lost their lives. The vessel had been moored at the same spot since late January. Her purpose had been to defend American interests during the civil war that Cuba was fighting against Spain.

The United States became actively involved when news reached the mainland that a Spanish mine had dumped the *Maine* into Havana Harbor. Six weeks later war was declared. "Remember the *Maine!*" became the battle cry of the war.

Several inspections of the ship were made from 1898 to 1911. It wasn't until the 1911 Board of Inspection Report that the real fate of the *Maine* was determined. The ship had been submerged for 13 years and during those 13 years, various salvage operations had been carried out. But when they inspected the ship in 1911, it was in the open air. A cofferdam was built and the *Maine* was dewatered. Every bit of the wreckage was accurately identified. The displacements were measured and photographs were taken.

A complete and thorough investigation of the ship was made. And when experts now observe the photographs of the wreckage, with hull side and whole deck structures peeled back, it leaves no doubt.

The explosion that sank our ship and catapulted us into the Spanish-American War, was caused by a blast from twenty thousand pounds of powder—from the inside.

* * *

INAUSPICIOUS BEGINNING

The first person ever to be a passenger in an airplane

died while flying with Orville Wright. On September 17, 1908, Wright and Lt. Thomas Selfridge, of the U.S. Signal Corps, took off on a flight from Fort Meyer, Virginia. The plane's propeller snapped midway through the trip, and the plane plummeted 150 feet to the ground. Wright was hospitalized and Selfridge was killed.

World War I

BOSCHES GO HOME!

When Woodrow Wilson died in Washington on February 3, 1924, the German Embassy did not lower the flag to half mast. But on the day of the funeral, it was lowered properly and the ambassador resigned in a state of hysteria, after a crowd of war veterans had nailed the Stars and Stripes to the front door of the building and paraded up and down in the street before it singing *The Star-Spangled Banner*.

* * *

THE EMPTY BLUE YONDER

At the outbreak of World War I, the American Air Force consisted of only 50 men.

* * *

THEY NEEDED A SLOGAN

Kleenex tissues were originally manufactured as gas mask filters in World War I.

* * *

95

WAR NOT GAY

During World War I homosexuals in the French army were executed. The offender was allowed a final charge against the enemy if he was an officer, providing that he would get himself shot.

* * *

HENRY FORD'S PEACE SHIP

The car manufacturer, Henry Ford, chartered the *Oscar II* for a peace crusade to Europe in December of 1915. Ford's slogan was, "Get the boys out of the trenches by Christmas."

Ford's involvement in opposition to the war seems to have begun in the spring of 1915. He made statements to the press denouncing the conflict in bitterest terms, claiming the war was a capitalist war brought on by the money lenders and Wall Street parasites; later he began to name names, including Morgan and Company for its half-billion-dollar loan to the Allies. If the war spread to the United States, he said he would burn his factory rather than fill an order for cars that might be put to military use.

Ford's idea for translating his sentiments into action was the outcome of a long interview that fall with the Hungarian journalist and suffrage organizer, Rosika Schwimmer. Schwimmer was touring the country in behalf of an international peace movement. When the subject of a conference of neutrals to be held in some non-belligerent country was suggested to him, Ford declared his willingness to finance such a plan.

The *Oscar II* left New York for Christina, Norway,

and from there the delegates went to Stockholm, where the conference was formally set up on January 26, 1916. Ford did not stay for the parley. Confined to his stateroom with a bad cold for much of the trip, he went to bed on arrival, and a few days later, under the pressure of several of his friends who had opposed the entire venture, sailed for home.

In January 1917, reflecting a change in public opinion, Ford's enthusiasm began to abate. A month later, he announced that his support for the conference would end March 1. When war was declared on April 6, his pacifism was dissolved. By October he was urging everyone to "back our Uncle Samuel with a shotgun loaded to the muzzle with buckshot."

* * *

NO THANK YOU, ONE SCIENTIST IS ENOUGH

A delegation of representatives of scientific groups went to Washington when the United States entered World War I to formally offer their services to the U.S. Navy. The delegation was politely received, heard and asked to return the following day for an answer. They did so, and were told, "No thank you. The Navy already has a scientist."

* * *

IN THE WRONG PLACE AT THE WRONG TIME

A German spy in World War I, Peter Karpin, was captured by the French as soon as he entered the country in 1914. Faked reports were sent by the French in his name to Germany and his wages and expense money were intercepted. Finally Karpin escaped in 1917. With Karpin's intercepted money a Frenchman bought a car and was driving into the occupied Ruhr, when he ran over and killed a man; that man was Peter Karpin.

* * *

FREEDOM OF SPEECH

Congress passed wartime laws against espionage and sedition that established heavy penalties for criticizing the government, the Constitution, the flag, the uniforms of the Army and Navy, any Allied nation, or for obstructing the sale of United States War Bonds. Under these laws an offender could be fined up to $10,000 and/or receive 200 years in prison for advocating a reduced production of war necessities or for saying anything "disloyal, profane, scurrilous, or abusive" about any aspect of the government or the war effort. A supplementary court decision forbade historians to disagree in any way with the official explanation of the causes of World War I, which held that Germany had been entirely at fault.

So zealously prosecuted were these laws, which clearly violated the spirit of the First Amendment, that about 6,000 people were arrested and 1,500 sentenced, many for simply criticizing the Red Cross or the YMCA. The producer of a film entitled *The Spirit of '76* served three years in prison for showing British soldiers killing American women and children during the American Revolution.

* * *

CRAMPED QUARTERS

During World War I, a British soldier hid from the Germans in a cupboard for four years.

Patrick Fowler of the 11th Hussars was cut off from his regiment at the Battle of Le Cateau early in the war. Wearing a borrowed civilian coat, he wandered along the French countryside in an effort to evade the Germans. He met a woodcutter who took him to his mother-in-law's house. Fowler was hidden in a wardrobe less than six feet high. He never left his refuge except for a few minutes each night to stretch and eat.

Eight German soldiers were later billeted in the house, but they never bothered to open the cupboard.

When the owner of the house moved, Fowler was transported to her new house in the cupboard. A German soldier helped lift the cupboard and made no mention of its weight.

The Germans retreated in the winter of 1918. After four years Fowler was able to leave his cramped hiding place. The cupboard is now on display at the Imperial War Museum in England.

* * *

TAKE HIM, HE'S YOURS

Lenin was on a walking tour in the Dolomites when World War I broke out. He was imprisoned and might have been shot as a Russian spy by the Austrians if the Socialist mayor of Vienna hadn't believed Lenin was a greater danger to the Russians than he was to Austrians.

* * *

LARGEST MUTINY

In World War I, 56 French divisions, comprising some 650,000 men and their officers, refused to obey orders of General Nivelle in April 1917 after the failure of his offensive.

* * *

WAR GAVE WIDE DISTRIBUTION TO A SWEET TREAT

The chocolate bar was not widely distributed until World War I, when chocolatiers shipped bars of solid chocolate to G.I.'s in training camps across the nation.

Manufacturers began to individually wrap chocolate "bars" because the weighing and cutting of smaller blocks became too time-consuming. Thus the chocolate bar, as we know it today, was born.

* * *

PRECIOUS REAL ESTATE

The British and French armies in World War I did not advance more than three miles at any point on the Western front in the whole year of 1915. The three miles cost the French Army alone near 1.5 million men.

* * *

LOOK OUT BELOW!

In 1915 a German bombardment dislodged a statue of the Madonna from on top of Albert Cathedral in France. For three years the statue dangled precariously from its feeble support. Frenchmen insisted the war would end once the statue fell. The statue was finally blown to the ground by German shells on November 10, 1918—and the Armistice was signed the next day.

*   *   *

OFF INTO THE WILD BLUE YONDER AND BACK AGAIN

On January 6, 1918, an American, Captain J.H. Hedley, was flying 15,000 feet over German territory in a plane piloted by a Canadian named Makepeace. The craft was suddenly attacked by German fighters. In an effort to evade the enemy, Makepeace took his plane into a nearly vertical dive. Hedley, shocked by the sudden maneuver was pulled out of his seat and off into the ozone.

Giving his comrade up for lost, Makepeace rapidly descended several hundred feet before leveling off. Then amazingly, Hedley landed on the tail of the airplane! The steep dive evidently created a strong suction in which the captain was caught.

Hanging on to the tail of the plane with all his might, Hedley finally managed to climb back into his seat. The plane landed safely behind Allied lines and the American captain emerged shaken but grateful to be alive.

*   *   *

WEIGHTED ODDS

During World War I, the odds against a French or German soldier being killed were 5 to 1, which meant that one out of every five Frenchmen and Germans who served in that war was killed.

* * *

BUDDY BUDDY

Before the outbreak of World War I, a person with whom another chummed was called his buddy. The term became so common in this sense among the soldiers in the war that it gradually came to be applied to former soldiers in general. An artificial flower sold for the benefit of veterans is called a buddy poppy.

* * *

NO U.S. PLANES ALLOWED

The U.S. Army's interest in aeronautics goes back to the captive balloons used during the Civil War. Interest in heavier-than-air flying equipment, powered by the internal combustion engine, began even before a successful flight was made. The War Department subsidized Dr. Samuel P. Langley's flight experiments in 1898, but withdrew its support in 1903 when his ill-fated plane crashed in the Potomac River. Perhaps because of Langley's failure, Wilber and Orville Wright's machine was not given a chance to pass Army tests until late in 1908. The test results of the Wrights' aircraft indicated that the Army had a promising new weapon within its grasp. But when Congress was asked for funds to further its development, the request was denied. In the meantime other nations were paying attention to the new weapon that was to influence warfare so profoundly. By 1913 Russia, Germany, France and England were spending millions annually on aviation. Even Mexico was spending $400,000 yearly at a time when the United States was devoting only $125,000.

Congress authorized the creation of an Aviation Section in the Signal Corps in July, 1914. Sixty officers and 260 enlisted men comprised the group. But little was accomplished because the air enthusiasts received only grudging and tardy support from their superiors.

When the United States entered World War I, the Army had been left behind in aviation, not only in equipment but in organization and indoctrination as well. U.S. pilots were required to learn as they fought in foreign aircraft. The country that had the first successful airplane flight did not have a single American-made fighter plane reach the Western front before the Armistice, despite the millions of dollars poured into the effort in order to catch up with other powers.

* * *

THE TWO MISSING FINGERS

In 1915, E.G. Steele of Weybridge, England, was a gunner in the R.A.F. While serving he was tried and punished for striking an officer, and sentenced to ten days Number One punishment. Steele was tied to a gunwheel for one hour at sundown as part of the punishment. An Australian brigade passed through Steele's camp that evening on their way to a nearby French town. On the first day of the sentence, they noticed him tied to the wheel. They crowded around Steele and asked the guard what was going on. After being told, one of the Australians stepped forward and quickly cut him loose. They called a meeting between the officers of both units, and to avoid further trouble it was decided that that part of Steele's sentence should be postponed for the time being.

Steele noticed that the man who cut him loose had two missing fingers on his left hand. Ten years later, Steele was travelling on the New York subway. The man sitting next to him asked Steele for directions in an Australian accent. Steele began telling him of the above incident that happened in France. The man finished the story for Steele and held up his left hand; it had two missing fingers.

*   *   *

SELF-PORTRAIT

The model for Uncle Sam in the famous "I want you" poster of World War I was the artist who designed the poster, James Montgomery Flagg.

*   *   *

FIRST AMERICAN ACE

Captain Eddie Rickenbacker shot down more enemy aircraft than any other American pilot during World War I. But he was not the first to become an American Ace.

In his autobiography *Rickenbacker*, he mentions several men who were already aces when he started combat flying in France in the spring of 1918. Raoul

Lufbery was one mentioned, and was described by Rickenbacker as "The American ace of aces."

Rickenbacker shot down twenty-five enemy aircraft. According to the account in his autobiography, "Rickenbacker" was originally "Rickenbacher"; Rickenbacker changed the "h" to a "k" in order to minimize its Germanic origin.

* * *

HE CAPTURED 132 GERMAN PRISONERS BY HIMSELF

On October 8, 1918, a small group of American soldiers were surrounded by Germans in the Argonne Forest of France. Command was passed by the wounded sergeant of the troop to a young corporal named Alvin York. The boy from Fentress County, Tennessee, did not surrender even though capture seemed imminent. Flattening his body against a tree, York fired; 12 Germans fell in quick succession. Astonished and furious, eight Germans charged down a hill toward the lone American soldier. Firing eight times, York killed them all. The other Germans not realizing that they had surrounded only a handful of Americans, thought they were outnumbered. Abandoning their positions, they soon surrendered.

York had captured 92 prisoners. The six Americans in York's command were vastly outnumbered by their prisoners. To fool the enemy, York marched the prisoners ahead of him and his troops toward American lines. Whenever they came to another German machine-gun nest, the gunners assumed that a large army battalion followed the group of prisoners. When York reached the American lines, he had captured 132 prisoners and put 35 machine-gun nests out of action. He later received the highest governmental awards from France and the U.S.

World War II

HITLER'S SIGN

Few ominous experiences caused the superstitious Hitler more concern than the one that occurred when he was about to lay the cornerstone of a Munich art gallery on October 15, 1933. After the chairman had stated that the ceremony was the "sign and symbol of the future of the Nazi movement," Hitler stepped forward and, in delivering the first blow on the stone, broke the silver hammer in two. Obviously extremely shocked and upset, he resumed his seat without uttering a single word.

* * *

THE ORIGIN OF THE TERM "NAZI"

The term Nazi as applied to the followers of Adolf Hitler, is a phonetic spelling of the first two syllables of Nationalsozialist Deutche Arbeiter-Partie, which is German for German National Socialist Party, and was adopted as the official name of the Hitler organization. The full name of the party was too difficult for the average person to pronounce, so a shortened name was used to advocate and popularize the cause.

* * *

FIRST SHOTS IN WORLD WAR II

Although World War II was officially started on September 1, 1939, when Hitler's forces invaded Poland, the first shots were fired 6 days earlier.

On August 26, a unit led by Lt. Albert Herzner captured the strategic Janlunkuv Pass in Poland, along with the railway station at Mosty and a small number of Polish prisoners.

Hitler had ordered 16 combat units to attack Poland, but called off the attack at the last minute.

The combat teams were radioed and summoned home, but none could be reached.

When Herzner telephoned central headquarters after his attack, he was told that the plans had been called off. On orders, he released his prisoners and came home.

Incredibly, the Polish let the incident pass without notice. The Poles were taken by surprise when the Nazis invaded on September 1st.

* * *

FIRST DEATHS IN WORLD WAR II

The first U.S. deaths in World War II weren't at Pearl Harbor. On October 31, 1941, more than a month earlier, a German U-boat torpedoed the U.S. destroyer *Reuben James* in the North Atlantic, killing more than 100 people.

* * *

THE JAPANESE DID NOT FIRE THE FIRST SHOTS AT PEARL HARBOR

The Japanese sneak attack on the United States naval base at Pearl Harbor, Hawaii, almost destroyed America's Pacific Fleet. Yet, the first shot at Pearl Harbor was fired by the United States, not Japan.

A small American minesweeper signaled the U.S. World War I destroyer *Ward* just before daybreak December 7, 1941. An unidentified submarine was sighted heading toward Pearl Harbor. Nearly four hours later, the *Ward's* lookouts sighted the conning tower of a green, two-man midget submarine trailing behind an American supply ship. The skipper of the *Ward*, Lt. William W. Outerbridge, called his crew to their battle stations. "Commence fire!" he ordered. A shell from the no. 3 gun blasted the conning tower of the midget submarine when it was 50 yards away. The stricken sub spun crazily, erupted and sank. The first shots of Pearl Harbor had been fired at 6:45 a.m.; the United States had fired them. Their victim, a Japanese submarine, which was to have been part of the planned attack.

* * *

YOU CAN'T TRUST RADAR

Radar was a new technology in 1941, and wasn't entirely trusted. So the privates on duty at the Opana radar station of the U.S. 55th Signal Aircraft Warning service were advised not to be concerned when radar picked up incoming craft at 136 miles. It was decided that the planes must be U.S. planes due from the mainland. The day was December 7, 1941, and the aircraft sighted on radar near Hawaii's Kahuku Point turned out to be the vanguard of Japan's "wild eagles"—353 carrier-based warplanes that were to sink or heavily damage eighteen U.S. warships in Pearl Harbor and kill 2,303 men.

* * *

YOUR WARNING MESSAGE IS A LITTLE LATE

Chief of Staff General George C. Marshall, in Washington sent a message advising island defense forces to be on alert. The message was sent through commercial channels and received by U.S. Army and Naval commanders in Hawaii. The message was sent five hours after the Japanese had successfully launched a surprise air strike on Pearl Harbor.

* * *

WHERE WERE YOU WHEN THE BOMBS FELL?

At 2:20 p.m. Washington time, 55 minutes after the bombs fell on Pearl Harbor, White House Press Secretary Steve Early, at home in pajamas, got the press services simultaneously on the phone and released the news.

On the bridge of the *U.S.S. Ramapo*, a commander banged away at the planes with a pistol. Tears flowed down his cheeks. A bosun's mate frantically threw wrenches at the low flying aircraft. From the magazine came a call asking what he needed. "Powder," he yelled. "I can't keep throwing things at them."

Refusing to issue ammunition, a sergeant in the 27th

Infantry at Pearl pointed to a sign that said no ammunition without captain's orders.

Christian Science Monitor correspondent Joseph Harsch was awakened by the explosions while in a Honolulu hotel. He thought the sounds were much like the air raids in Berlin, where he had been the year before. Waking his wife, he said: "Darling, you've often asked what an air raid sounds like. Listen to this—it's a good imitation." "Oh, so that's what it's like," she said. Then they both rolled over and went back to sleep.

The gunners on the *U.S.S. Argonne* shot down their own antenna.

Battery B on Oahu was issued machine gun ammunition dated 1918—so old the belts fell apart in the loading machines.

Near the married men's quarters at Pearl, a group of children jumped up and down screaming, "Here come the Indians."

Dashing to get a better look at the bombing, a Honolulu man yelled at a reporter: "The Mainland papers will exaggerate this."

People in Phoenix phoned *The Arizona Republic* newsroom and asked: "Have you got any score on the game between the Chicago Bears and the Cardinals? Aren't you getting anything besides that war stuff?"

Ernest Vogt and his family continued eating their Sunday chicken dinner in New York City: "I thought it was another Orson Welles hoax."

At nightfall, a sentry at Schofield Barracks near Pearl, challenged three times, got no answer and shot one of his own mules.

*   *   *

WATCH THAT BIRD!

Instructions on how to escape the attack of large birds were issued to British pilots in 1934. One noteworthy attack occurred near Allahabad, India, when two eagles attempted to "kill" a low-flying three-engined plane. One bird flew straight into the middle propeller while the other, diving from about 10,000 feet, crashed through the steel wing, making a large hole.

* * *

UNTIL WE MEET AGAIN

In 1943 M/sgt. John Hassebrock received a three-day pass to marry a WAC corporal just before he went overseas. He and his bride lost track of each other until one night in France when he was in a convoy to the front lines. Stopping at a farmhouse to spend the night, he saw his wife again—on the exact day and hour of their first wedding anniversary.

* * *

WORLD WAR II GIRLPOWER

Girlpower was a vital part of America's wartime strength during World War II. In the five months after Pearl Harbor, 750,000 women volunteered for duty at armament plants. At first, managers in heavy industry were suspicious of using women workers, and only 80,000 of the early volunteers won prompt assignment. But by 1944, some 3.5 million women stood side by side with six million men on the assembly lines, turning out entire cargo ships in 17 days, reducing the time needed to make a bomber from 200,000 man-hours to 13,000. In the process they helped win the coveted Army-Navy "E" pennant for excellence in meeting awesome weapons quotas. Hitler's propaganda minister, Joseph Goebbels, refused to acknowledge the overwhelming triumphs of U.S. war production and on a note of sour grapes made the following statement:

"The Americans are so helpless that they must fall back again and again upon boasting about their materiel. Their loud mouths produce a thousand airplanes and tanks almost daily, but when they need them they haven't got them and are therefore taking one beating after another."

*   *   *

POOR ADOLF

"I think it's pretty obvious that this war is no pleasure for me. For five years I have been separated from the rest of the world. I haven't been to a theatre, I haven't heard a concert, and I haven't seen a movie."—Adolf Hitler.

*   *   *

WORLD WAR II'S WOMEN PILOTS

The Women's Air Force Service Pilots (WASPs) went through officers' training during World War II and were subject to military discipline. They lived in military barracks and wore GI uniforms (which they called "zoot suits"). Although they were promised military commissions, the WASPs were disbanded after the war without having attained military status and veterans' benefits.

Between September 1942 and December 1944, more than 1,000 women were accepted into the WASPs. H.H. "Hap" Arnold, Commanding General of the Army Air Forces, enthusiastically supported the women pilots. The WASPs ferried fighter and bomber planes to points of embarkation in the United States and Canada. They towed targets for combat pilots' practice shooting, and performed other duties to free male pilots for combat. A branch chief for the Federal Aviation Administration and former WASP, Margaret Boylan, stated, "They worked seven days a week, sunup to sundown."

Several attempts to pass legislation in the WASPs' behalf failed, despite efforts by Senator Barry Goldwater, their sponsor on Capitol Hill. Goldwater flew with WASP ferry pilots during the war and said their performance was equal to or better than that of their male counterparts. In November, 1977, President Carter signed into law a bill giving the former World War II women pilots the legal status of other World War II veterans.

* * *

RUSSIA'S WOMEN FIGHTER PILOTS

In World War II, Russian women pilots were assigned to combat units. Three aviation regiments were "manned" solely by female personnel in 1941. The 586th Women's Fighter Regiment defended its combat route efficiently and no enemy bombers reached the Soviet Union's protected industrial centers and railway junctions. Orders and medals of the U.S.S.R. were awarded to the entire personnel of the regiment.

Following are a list of some of the women fighter pilots, according to the *Soviet Military Review* (March 1977):

Raya Surnachevskaya and Tamara Pamyatnykh. In a battle over a large railway junction and a bridge over the River Don, they engaged 42 enemy bombers. Against terrific odds they shot down four bombers, breaking up the attack; not a single bomb hit the objective they were covering.

Lily Litvyak and Katya Budanova were members of ace teams carrying out "lone-wolf" operations. Litvyak destroyed 12 enemy planes and Budanova 10. Both women were awarded the Order of the Red Banner and the Order of the Patriotic War.

Valeria Ivanovna Khomyakova was the first woman pilot in the history of aviation to shoot down an enemy bomber. She destroyed a German Junkers-88, in September 1942, over Saratov on the Volga.

Katherine I. Zeleko encountered seven Messerschmitt Me-109s. It was her thirteenth dog fight, and with all odds against her, she shot down one of the fighters. She was attacking a second when her plane was hit and nose-dived to the ground. Her heart was pierced by a cannon splinter.

* * *

PRAYER FOR PEACE

During February, 1944, in Delhi, India, the Hindus attempted to bring about the end of World War II by a mass prayer service known as a Mahayajna, the first one they had deemed necessary since the 17th century. Around 100 sacred fires, 1,000 Hindu priests prayed six hours a day for ten days, reciting 10,800,000 prayers in this ceremony which cost more than $500,000.

* * *

THE U.S. CONCENTRATION CAMP

At the beginning of World War II, fear took many irrational forms, from the merely ludicrous to the unspeakably cruel. "Enemy aliens" of German and Italian birth were rounded up by the Justice Department at the beginning of the war. In all about 3,000 Germans and less than a hundred Italians were "detained."

Anxieties and political pressure were felt because of Japanese victories in the Pacific. On February 19, 1942, President Roosevelt signed Executive Order 9066 to deal with the Japanese problem on the West Coast.

Bigotry drowned out the voice of reason, led by the Hearst Press and the Western Growers Protective Association, a pressure group of California Agriculturists who coveted the farmland owned by Japanese Americans.

Lieutenant General John L. De Witt, head of Western Defense Command, had distinguished himself when he announced the presence of "30 Japanese planes over San Francisco Bay," thus causing some panic but even more derision. De Witt, however, stuck to his story. Enforcement of Executive Order 9066 fell into his hands. He was determined to protect his command from the wily "Jap." The fact that nothing had happened that couldn't be handled did not deter him: "The very fact that no sabotage has taken place is a disturbing and confirming indication that such action will be taken," he stated.

On March 39, 1942, De Witt issued his own Civilian Exclusion Order No. 20, pertaining to persons of Japanese ancestry. During April and May more than 110,000 Japanese-American citizens were rounded up and shipped to detention camps. (Once Roosevelt inadvertently used the term "concentration camp.")

The camps were crowded, depressing, and demeaning. Protests from the American Civil Liberties Union and others finally succeeded in the closing of these camps by the end of 1944. But the psychological scars from the experience remained with the prisoners for years afterward.

* * *

PRIORITIES

The U.S. War Department was urged by the War Refugee Board to bomb the industrial installations and mass-extermination equipment at the infamous Nazi concentration camp at Auschwitz during World War II. But the plea was rejected because it would be "an unwarranted diversion of planes needed elsewhere."

* * *

THE NAZI EMPIRE

Nazi Germany and its allies by 1942 controlled a larger portion of Continental Europe than had ever been held by any single nation in history—including the Roman Empire! At that time only neutral Spain, Sweden, Switzerland, Portugal and parts of European Russia were not in German control.

* * *

WORLD'S LARGEST OFFICE BUILDING

Not long before America's entry into World War II, the construction of a building to house all the agencies of the U.S. War Department was proposed by General B.B. Sommervell. Many people felt the proposal was an unnecessary extravagance for a nation that might soon become embroiled in a world war. But others felt this was precisely the reason why the erection of centralized offices was imperative.

The construction of the building began in September, 1941, on a 34-acre site across the Potomac River from Washington, D.C. More than 13,000 workers were employed on the giant project; six million cubic yards of earth were moved; 41,492 pillars were sunk into the marshy earth; 410,000 cubic yards of concrete were poured; and 680,000 tons of sand and gravel were dredged from the bottom of the Potomac. War Department workers began moving into the building even before it was completed in January 1943.

Today the Pentagon is synoymous with American military might and is the largest office building in the world. Its total floor area could fill a square whose sides are one-half mile long. The building consists of 5 concentric pentagons connected by 10 "spokes." The outermost pentagon extends 921 feet on each of its five sides. The innermost pentagon encloses a large open courtyard. Paved courts and roads for delivering vehicles separate other rings. The ingenious design of the building assures that, despite its size, no two offices are more than 1,800 feet—or six minutes walking time—from each other.

Truly a city in itself, the Pentagon contains five stories plus a mezzanine and basement comprising a total area of 6½ million square feet—three times the floor area of the Empire State Building. Each day, the Pentagon houses 30,000 Defense Department workers.

The total cost of the Pentagon, $83 million, was considered astronomical at the time of its construction. Yet today, the rental of office space of equal size would cost the government more than $20 million each day!

* * *

ORDERED FROM THE WISH BOOK

General George Patton ordered spare parts for several hundred U.S. Army tanks from Sears, Roebuck and Co., on the eve of America's entry into World War II.

Patton arrived at Fort Benning, Ga., in 1940 as a brigade commander with the 2nd Armored Division. He'd hoped to organize a tank unit capable of taking on Hitler's panzer divisions. His hopes were soon dashed by the sorry state of the 325 tanks he found at Fort Benning. Most were in serious disrepair, some were badly rusted and had missing parts. Orders for replacement parts went unfilled.

Patton was informed by one of his mechanics that whenever he needed parts and was unable to get them from official channels, he ordered them from Sears. Patton seized on the idea and ordered the necessary parts, paying for them with his personal checks. He ordered not only parts for the tanks, but also for hundreds of other military vehicles. Sears delivered the parts, and Patton was never reimbursed.

* * *

AIR BASES MADE OF ICE

In the early years of World War II, German U-boats were sinking thousands of tons of shipping every month. The usual form of protection was escort warships. But the best defense of all against submarine attack was aircraft patrol.

Air cover was limited to within only a few hundred miles of friendly Atlantic coasts at the time. Aircraft did not have the vast flying ranges and flight-refueling techniques of today.

In 1942, Geoffrey Pike, an English inventor, proposed a possible solution: giant, manmade icebergs that could be used as floating mid-Atlantic airstripes. These might also be used as halfway refueling stops when ferrying new airplanes from the United States.

Pike's project was named Habakkuk, after a minor prophet in the Old Testament. Habakkuk 1:5 says: "For I am doing a work in your days that you would not believe if told." Pike's ice ship was designed to be 300 feet wide and 2,000 feet long—a hollow ice hull like a rectangular box. Aircraft would land on the upper surface, beneath which would be hangers, workshops, crews' quarters, and a refrigeration plant.

Lakes in the Canadian province of Alberta were used for secret research work on the project. It was discovered that the addition of 10 percent wood pulp in small-scale prototypes made the ice as strong as concrete and as easy to work with as wood.

But there was one big problem. When it was found

that Habakkuk would cost at least as much to build as a conventional aircraft carrier, enthusiasm waned, and the project was abandoned.

* * *

PUZZLING THE ENGLISH

The Germans recognized the English penchant for the crossword puzzle, during World War II. In a propaganda ploy, Germans showered England with leaflets containing crossword puzzles. A typical clue might be *Warmonger*, with "Roosevelt" or "Churchill" as the answer.

* * *

KEEP IT DOWN, C.B.

During the 1940's, sounds of shellfire and other explosions in war movies had to be greatly reduced, sometimes to as little as one-hundredth of their actual volume, so they would not ruin the theater projector or deafen the audience.

* * *

HITLER'S HIDEOUT

Probably the most incredible mistake made by the Nazis in France was the building and furnishing of a stupendous subterranean headquarters and hideout which they never used. Constructed north of Soissons between 1940 and 1943, the secret city was fifty feet below the ground, occupied twenty-five square miles and had living accommodations for 100,000 men, including electric lights, showers and bus service. To deceive Allied airmen, the fields on the surface were camouflaged with numerous farmhouses and bomb-damaged buildings—all made of cardboard.

* * *

HEIL TONTO!

The sale of Navajo blankets almost ceased during World War II. The reason for the decline was that the ancient Navajo symbol for the sun, woven into most of the blankets, looked exactly like Hitler's swastika.

* * *

NAZI BOMBS PLANTED ON THE U.S. COAST

In the dark hours of June 13, 1942, a rubber boat slipped out of the fog onto the beach at Amagansett, Long Island, and discharged four men and four stout crates. Four nights later, on a beach in Florida, another sub discharged four more men with similar boxes.

The mission of the men was accomplished, the burying of explosives. The four men who planted the explosives were Nazi saboteurs—the vanguard of Hitler's secret invasion of the United States. The bombs were to be used against American factories, bridges, stores, and water supplies.

The Nazi saboteurs might have succeeded in their mission had they been better trained and less fanatical. But one of the men, George Dasch, lost his nerve and surrendered to the FBI the second day. Using information supplied by Dasch, agents quickly captured the entire crew before they had even begun to plan their first raid.

The men were tried by a U.S. military tribunal. Dasch and Ernest Peter Burger were given prison terms (President Truman pardoned both in 1948), the other six men were electrocuted.

The arrest of the spies was highly publicized, but trial proceedings were kept secret. Hitler thought the saboteurs' early detection was a result of American counterintelligence. He soon abandoned plans for similar missions.

* * *

MacARTHUR WAS HERE

The name General Douglas MacArthur is required by Philippine law to be forever shouted out at parade roll calls of the Philippine Army—and there should always be an answer.

MacArthur made a promise when the Japanese forced him off the islands in 1942. He made a famous vow: "I shall return." After two years of deadly island fighting, he and his troops made good his promise in October, 1944.

An appreciative Philippine Congress, nine months later, resolved: "That in reverent appreciation of General Douglas MacArthur, his name be carried in perpetuity on the Company rolls of the units of the Philippine Army and, at parade roll calls, when his name is called, the senior noncommissioned officer, shall answer, 'Present in Spirit.'" Hearing of this, MacArthur cried as he had not done since childhood.

* * *

CRAB LIGHT

During World War II, Japanese soldiers had an ingenious method of producing an undedectable light. The
remains of tiny crabs that produced their own biological
light as the result of enzyme action were dried out and
ground into a powder. When water was added to the
powder held in a soldier's hands, a faint blue light was
produced and the soldiers could read maps at night
without attracting attention.

* * *

POKER FACE NICK

During World War II, in the South Pacific, on Green
Island, a great deal of money passed hands in poker
games. The Navy officers who played lost a great deal
of money to a lieutenant named Nick. Nick rarely lost
at poker. And, even more remarkable, before being
assigned to Green Island, he had never played poker
before in his life!

There wasn't a lot of action on Green Island except
for occasional Japanese bombing raids. The men had
lots of time for nightly poker games.

A SCAT taught Nick the basics of poker. Nick
seemed to have a natural aptitude for the game, and
that genius soon gained him a reputation throughout
the South Pacific.

His "poker face" was credited as being the reason for
many of his high winnings. He once bluffed a lieutenant
commander out of fifteen hundred dollars—with a pair
of deuces.

Nick's wartime winnings came to about thirty-five

hundred dollars. The money was used to invest in a political career. Old Poker Face, Richard Nixon, later became President of the United States.

* * *

FOLDERS HO!

The Allies used 125,000,000 different maps in preparing their plans for invasion of Europe through France during World War II.

* * *

THE REST WERE IN THE ARMY

Hitler's SS, or Black Guards, maintained three great military and espionage branches with a total of about 8,000,000 members. The first consisted of a military force that guarded prison camps, handled mass executions and stood ready to crush revolts. The second trained men for farm, fire, political and other organizations, even the Red Cross. The third comprised a vast group of workers in stores, factories, hotels and restaurants who spied on and reported any anti-Nazi talk among their friends, associates and patrons.

* * *

WATCH OUT, WE'RE COMING

Nazi soldiers in control of French cities often neglected to sound an alert for the inhabitants when bombers were approaching. To rectify this R.A.F. planes flew over a town twenty minutes before an Allied air raid and sounded its own special siren to warn and give the people sufficient time to take shelter.

* * *

I APOLOGIZE FOR BEING ALIVE

Japanese recruits were taught during World War II to fight until killed. Those who lived through the war and returned to civilian life felt that they did not fulfill their duty and generally developed a sense of humility. Therefore, when an ex-soldier wrote a book, he began it with an abject apology for being alive.

* * *

A GOOD WAC NEVER GETS PWOP

To free able-bodied servicemen for active duty, in May 1942 Secretary of War Stimson authorized a publisher from Texas, Oveta Culp Hobby, to form a Women's Army Auxiliary Corps, later known as the WAC. Male reporters at Mrs. Hobby's first press conference bombarded her with irreverent questions. "Can officer WACs date privates?" the newsmen asked. "Will WACs' underwear be khaki?" "What if an unmarried WAC gets pregnant?" The next day and for months to come the papers carried stories about a petticoat army, wackies and powder magazines.

The press had just as good a time with the Navy's WAVES, the Coast Guard's SPARS and the women Marines; and the embattled servicewomen got no support from their military brothers. One soldier, writing his sister in order to persuade her not to enlist, asked. "Why can't these gals just stay home and be their own sweet little selves, instead of being patriotic?"

In spite of all the boos and catcalls, the women in uniform performed efficiently in posts from Boston to Bataan, and contrary to the newsmen's mock concern, almost never got PWOP (pregnant without permission). Replacing badly needed manpower, the ladies worked as airplane mechanics, cooks, code clerks, and female pilots who ferried planes to Europe. In all, more than 300,000 girls served.

* * *

QUICK AS A WINK

In 1943, the Navy adopted a new system of training its men to recognize ships and planes instantly from a glimpse of their total image, instead of identification of their distinctive parts. The course consisted of a 120-hour study of 2,000 pictures of 168 objects from various angles on slides that were run through a projector at high speeds. To pass, a man had to identify a ship in one second and a plane in 1/75 of a second.

* * *

WE'LL LEAVE IT IN THE SAME CONDITION WE FOUND IT

In the winter of 1943, in England, 3,000 inhabitants of eight villages and 180 farms, occupying 25 square miles in South Devon, complied with the request of their government to move away so that American troops could use the area for six months as a training ground for the invasion of France. As these "Normandy rehearsals" were live-ammunition battles, most of the houses, churches, shops and lands in the area were so wrecked that it took years for the returning inhabitants to restore them to anything like their former condition.

* * *

AMERICAN KAMIKAZES

In January of 1942, a Pennsylvania surgeon named L.S. Adams arrived in Washington with an idea for a U.S. suicide squadron.

FDR quickly gave his approval for the military operation. On direct orders from the White House, operation X Ray began.

The American Kamikazes were to be paratroopers with incendiary bombs wired to their chests and parachuted from bombers high over Japanese cities. The troopers were to guide themselves to vulnerable landmarks in the predawn dark.

After 20 months and 2 million dollars of preparation, the Army abandoned the operation in the fall of 1943. The only reason given was "solely on the basis of military considerations."

The suicide paratroopers who almost died for our cause—our American Kamikazes—were Mexican freetailed bats.

* * *

FIRST FEMALE BRONZE STAR WINNER

First Lieutenant Cordelia E. Cook was awarded the first Bronze Star to go to a woman. Cook was an Army nurse who served in direct support of combat operations from November 1943 to January 1944, when she was wounded. Despite her wounds she carried on her hospital duties. The Bronze Star was presented in May, 1944, by Major General Geoffrey Keys of the Fifth Army. Lieutenant Cook also received the Purple Heart, thus qualifying her as the first woman in World War II to win two decorations.

* * *

MIGHTY MOUSE

The heaviest tank ever built weighed 180 tons and stood almost 20 feet high. Its front armor was 12 inches thick. Code-named the Mouse, it first appeared in 1944, after the German Army's tank divisions had been badly mauled on the Russian front.

Hitler had no hope of matching the masses of Russian tanks ranged against his forces, so he briefed Dr. Porsche—designer of the Volkswagen Beetle—to invent a land battleship, a tank that could outdo any enemy tank, yet remain completely invulnerable to enemy fire due to massive armor protection.

Dr. Porsche produced the Mouse, powered with a 1,500-horsepower diesel engine driven by an electrical generator that fed power to two motors mounted in each hub of the monster's giant caterpillar tracks.

But its size and weight were the Mouse's biggest liability. Its top speed was only 12 miles an hour and when it was driven along roads on a test, the vibration cracked foundations, smashed cobblestone, and shattered windows in all the towns and villages it passed through; the pressure on its tracks was enough to cause it to sink into anything but the driest ground. Finally the project was dropped.

* * *

PROTECT THE PROPAGANDA

Bundles of Propaganda material dropped by Allied airmen prior to 1944 opened at great heights and were
scattered over vast rural areas by the wind. In 1944,
each bundle carried an inexpensive gadget, about the
size of a shoe-polish can, operated by barometric pressure, which held the sheets together until reaching a
low predetermined height, so they would not scatter
outside of the intended area.

* * *

MYSTERIOUS FIREBALLS OF WORLD WAR II

On November 23, 1944, crew members of an American bomber on a nighttime mission over Germany saw
some distant starlike points that became more clearly
visible as 10 or so balls of light that changed from
orange to red as they approached the plane. This was
the first of many reports of the mysterious fireballs that
appeared over Germany toward the end of World War
II.

Similar reports began to come from Germany and
then from the Pacific theater of war. The objects were
always described as glowing balls of orange, red or
white light, seemingly under intelligent control, that followed an aircraft for a while, then turned away and
disappeared from view.

After the war it was found that Japanese pilots also
encountered the phenomenon and assumed that it was
some secret American or Russian device used, perhaps,
to confuse radar. U.S. intelligence assumed that the

mysterious objects were of German make. Their true nature has never been determined.

*   *   *

MRS. TRUMAN DIDN'T SLEEP HERE

Harry S. Truman's mother, the daughter of an old-line Confederate family, had been briefly locked up in a Federal "internment camp" during the Civil War. Consequently she had no love for either President Lincoln or the U.S. Government. She came to visit Truman in the White House many years later and was offered the bedroom Lincoln had slept in. She said she'd rather sleep on the floor "than spend the night in the Lincoln bed."

At the age of 92, Mrs. Truman broke her hip and the President flew out to see her. Looking up from her bed of pain as he walked into the room, she said: "I don't want any smart cracks out of you. I saw your picture in the paper last week putting a wreath at the Lincoln Memorial."

*   *   *

FIRST MEDAL OF HONOR TO A CONSCIENTIOUS OBJECTOR

The first Medal of Honor awarded to a conscientious objector, was presented on October 12, 1945, by President Harry S. Truman to Private First Class Desmond T. Doss of Lynchburg, Va. Doss was given the Medal of Honor for outstanding bravery as a medical corpsman on Okinawa for specific acts between April 29 and May 21, 1945.

* * *

SAVED BY THE FLYING DUTCHMAN

When survivors of torpedoed ships and ditched planes could not be rescued in other ways during World War II, a U.S. Army Air Force plane dropped them by parachute a boat called the Flying Dutchman. Weighing 3,000 pounds and capable of holding about 36 people, the boat carried food, clothing, radio, fishing tackle and a large supply of gasoline. When the Dutchman struck water, a mechanism set off smokepots to mark the location and fired rockets which carried long buoy lines to assist survivors in reaching the boat.

* * *

DR. MORELL'S PRIZE PATIENT

Dr. Theodor Morell first saw the new patient for intestinal trouble. He offered his diagnosis and suggested treatment that included prescriptions of exotic bacteria, hormones, phosphorus, dextrose, belladonna . . . and strychnine. Not enough strychnine to kill the patient, of course.

The patient noticed an improvement in his condition in just a few weeks. His own words were: "What luck that I met Morell! He has saved my life. Wonderful, the way he has helped me!"

By Morell's own admission, his patient "was really never sick." Yet for money, prestige and for his sinister experimentation, the doctor continued "treatment."

The patient was given amphetamines—speed. The slightest patient complaint was answered by pills and injections. And the result was a shuffling, stumbling, trembling, emaciated, glassy-eyed, gray-complexioned shell of a man. He slept no more than three hours a night and in months appeared to age years.

The treatment lasted nine years—astounding, considering the quantities of atropine, strychnine and amphetamines consumed in that period of time.

Twenty-eight types of drugs in all. The speed took the highest toll.

The name of Dr. Theodor Morell has dropped into obscurity. Yet the name of the speed freak who spent the last decade of his life shattered and shaking will never be forgotten.

Hitler was "high."

* * *

POET IN A CAGE

Ezra Pound was kept in a cage by the United States Army at the Disciplinary Training Camp outside Pisa while awaiting trial for treason during World War II. The ungilded cage was made of steel, stood in the middle of the prison yard, had a tar-paper roof, bars all around, no covering, and was brightly lighted at night. Pound lived and wrote in his cage for six months, from May to October 1946. A guard was always stationed outside and none of the other prisoners were allowed to observe Pound.

* * *

SOLDIERS ON HORSEBACK

As recently as World War II, United States soldiers

rode into battle on horseback. President Ronald Reagan was a second lieutenant in the U.S. Cavalry reserve when the war broke out. Later he dismounted to join the First Motion Picture Unit of the Army Air Force.

The horse cavalry in this country dates back to the American Revolution, but it was going out of style by 1914, and only four horse cavalry regiments saw service in France in World War I. Horses were replaced with armored tanks after the war, which offered more mobility and firepower.

The 26th Cavalry regiment of the Philippine Scouts was the last mounted unit to see action. The 26th fired at invading Japanese forces in the Philippines in December 1941, and covered the American retreat to Bataan. On January 15, 1942, they made their last stand against the Japanese, then retreated to Bataan, where the men were forced to slaughter their horses for food.

* * *

STALIN'S OTHER SON

Joseph Stalin's son Jacob was captured during World War II. The Germans offered to exchange Jacob, but Stalin refused and his son died in a prison camp.

* * *

THE BAMBINO WAS NOT AMUSED

From their foxholes during World War II, American soldiers taunted their Japanese adversaries with biting references to the Emperor Hirohito. The Japanese frequently retorted with what they considered to be an ultimate insult to Americans: "To hell with Babe Ruth!"

* * *

ON THE ATOMIC BOMB

"That is the biggest fool thing we have ever done. The bomb will never go off, and I speak as an expert in explosives."—Admiral William Leahy to President Truman, 1945.

* * *

MOST DECORATED SOLDIER

Audie Murphy won fame as the most decorated soldier of World War II. He received 24 medals from the U.S. government, three from France, and one from Belgium. He later became a motion picture actor.

Audie Leon Murphy was born in rural Kingston, Texas, near Greenville. He enlisted in the Army in 1942 at age 18 and was appointed a second lieutenant in combat in 1944. Murphy served in North Africa and Europe. On January 26, 1945, German forces attacked his unit near Colmar, France. Murphy jumped on a burning tank destroyer and used its machine gun to kill about 50 enemy troops. He received the Medal of Honor, the nation's highest military award.

* * *

STATISTICS

More American men and women served in the Armed services in World War II than in any other war—over

16 million. More were killed or wounded in that war than in any other—more than 1 million.

*   *   *

MOST COSTLY WAR

The material cost of World War II far transcended that of the rest of history's wars put together and has been estimated at 1.5 trillion. The cost to the U.K. was five times as great as that of World War I. The total cost of World War II to the Soviet Union was estimated in May 1959 at $280 billion, while a figure of $530 billion has been estimated for the U.S.

*   *   *

SILHOUETTES OF TRAGEDY

The heat from the atomic bombs dropped on Hiroshima and Nagasaki in 1945 left an eerie legacy in time. Silhouette photographs from the victims and objects—some in the midst of movement—were printed upon buildings and roads as a result of the intense heat from the blasts.

The shadow of a human being sitting on the steps of a bank, looking toward the blast, is just one of the bizarre images. Another is of a shadow soldier unbuttoning his shirt after coming down a ladder from an observation post and hooking his sword to a clapboard. And in the shadow of a cart on a bridge, it is said, you can see the driver about to beat his horse.

*   *   *

LONGEST SERVING U.S. OFFICER

The longest serving U.S. officer was General of the Army Omar Nelson Bradley (1893–1981) who served 69 years in the army.

Bradley commanded the largest fighting force ever amassed in battle under the American flag. His troops swept through France, Belgium, The Netherlands, Germany, Austria, and Czechoslovakia during World War II. Bradley's Twelfth Army Group, later called the Central Group of Armies, consisted of the United States First, Third, Ninth, and Fifteenth armies. It numbered about 1,000,000 men, organized into more than 40 combat divisions.

*   *   *

BREAKFAST AT WILLOW RUN

During World War II, the United States government ordered the removal of air conditioning equipment from luxury stores, such as Tiffany's in New York, for use in war-related industrial plants. Unknown to toiling factory workers, they were being cooled by the same machines that had kept sweat from the brows of America's social elite in the jewel-bedecked aisles of Tiffany's.

*   *   *

YOU GO FIRST MR. DILLON

James Arness, the actor best known for his portrayal of U.S. Marshall Matt Dillon in the long-running series "Gunsmoke," was the first American soldier to jump off his boat at Anzio beachhead in World War II. He was ordered to do so because he was the tallest man in his

company and his commander wanted him to test the
depth of the water.

* * *

TOP OF THE CLASS

Only one famous general in United States history
ranked first in his graduating class at West Point—
Douglas MacArthur. Dwight Eisenhower, Omar Bradley, George Patton and William Westmoreland all failed
to finish within the top 45 students in their graduating
classes.

* * *

TO GIVE IS TO RECEIVE

Americans donated 13.3 million pints of blood in
Washington, D.C., during World War II.

Harry Starner, who had been wounded near Tarawa,
looked up from his hospital bed and saw his own name
as the donor on the label of the plasma bottle.

* * *

MY SON, THE WARRIOR

The parents of Dwight D. Eisenhower, who rose to
become one of the few five-star generals in U.S. history, were pacifists.

* * *

IS THERE A REAL DOCTOR IN THE HOUSE?

The first appendectomy ever performed aboard a submerged sub was not done by a doctor. During World

War II, a pharmacist's mate in the U.S. Navy performed a lifesaving appendectomy on a crewman in a submarine. His tools: a tea strainer, spoons and a homemade knife.

Seaman Darrel Dean Rector fell ill with acute appendicitis when his ship the *Seadragon* was on patrol in the Pacific, behind enemy lines. There was no doctor on board and the closest thing to a medical person was Pharmacist's Mate Wheeler B. Lipes, Jr., a lab technician by training who had witnessed an appendectomy.

Rector agreed to be operated on by Lipes because he faced certain death otherwise. Lipes had to improvise all his surgical instruments. A tea strainer was used to administer ether. Spoons bent at right angles kept the incision open during surgery. Alcohol from a torpedo was used to sterilize the instruments.

On September 11, 1942, the operation took place in the officer's wardroom with senior officers assisting. Lipes located the appendix, removed it and closed the incision, cutting the suture with a pair of fingernail scissors just as the ether ran out. Rector went back on duty 13 days later.

By war's end, ten other appendectomies were performed by amateurs using crude instruments. Each one was a success.

* * *

BOOZE BOATS

The Navy put out a bid for a pursuit-boat during World War II that would be so maneuverable it could turn on a dime. An ex-bootlegger, Andrew Higgins, turned in a plan within 48 hours. Recognizing it as a superb design, the Navy created the now-famous PT Boat. The blueprints for Higgins' design was based on a speedboat he had previously built for Prohibition rumrunners.

* * *

MAMA'S BOY

Mrs. MacArthur longed to say, "My son the General!" Douglas MacArthur's mother often sent persuasive letters to his army superiors suggesting it was time for her son to be promoted to general.

* * *

MADE IN JAPAN!

Nearly everyone is familiar with the photograph of the U.S. Marines raising the American flag at Iwo Jima.

Souvenir statuettes of the event were produced in volume. After examining one of the statues, U.S. Representative Charles S. Joelson (D., N.J.) complained vehemently and questioned the ethics of American businessmen. The statuettes being sold at the Iwo Jima Memorial in Washington, D.C., were made in Japan!

The famous photograph of the U.S. Marines raising the flag over Iwo Jima was staged. The flag was raised on February 23, 1945; later in the day the Marines had to raise it again for photographer Joe Rosenthal. The famous photo won Rosenthal a Pulitzer Prize.

* * *

SMILE, YOU'RE ON JAPANESE RADIO

A secret Japanese radio station was found operating underground in Hollywood during World War II.

Officials discovered the radio station because actress Lucille Ball had made a report. It seems that whenever she walked close to the area involved, she picked up Japanese radio broadcasts on some temporary fillings in her teeth.

*   *   *

WHITES ONLY

Blacks were not allowed to enlist in the United States Navy until World War II.

*   *   *

FORKED TONGUE

The Navajo language was used successfully as a code by the U.S. in World War II.

*   *   *

A SOLDIER'S RATION

A soldier's daily ration makes a small package; the U.S. Army's generous ration in World War II weighed only six pounds, that of the Japanese Army then, and of the North Vietnamese later, much less.

As late as 1864, in the Atlanta campaign of the U.S. Civil War, the Union Army's average daily ammunition requirement amounted to only one pound per man, as against three pounds for rations; Confederate forces were reported to expend, on the average, only half a cartridge per man.

* * *

DEATH BEFORE DISHONOR

In the early 1970's two Japanese soldiers emerged from the Pacific jungles to find the world almost unrecognizable since the end of their war a generation earlier.

In late January, 1972, Shoichi Yokoi was apprehended by fishermen on the island of Guam, where he and nine comrades had hidden when American troops landed in 1944. Yokoi's cohorts had eventually died or surrendered, but Yokoi had ignored a leaflet announcing his nation's surrender because, he said, "We Japanese soldiers were told to prefer death to the disgrace of getting captured alive."

Lt. Hiroo Onoda held out for two years longer, leaving the Philippine jungles on March 10, 1974. Unlike Yokoi, he had never been informed that World War II was over; when asked why he had not come out before, Onoda said, "I had not received the order." When both old soldiers returned to Japan, they were hailed as heroes.

* * *

THE BOMBING OF OREGON

It wasn't until many years after World War II that it was revealed that the U.S. Mainland had been bombed from the air for the first time. In September 1942, a Japanese plane flew over Oregon on two occasions and dropped bombs in an attempt to set the forests on fire. The submarine 1-25 carried the float-equipped plane across the Pacific. The general public assumed the forest fires of 1942 were started by firebombs carried in balloons by prevailing winds from Japan to Oregon.

This and That

FLYING THE U.S. NAVAL ENSIGN

U.S. Naval Regulations of 1865 stated that the ensign will be hoisted upon meeting, joining or falling in with other vessels at sea.

The 1893 Navy Regulations gave permission to deceive the enemy by flying false colors. This meant the flying of a neutral country's ensign in an attempt to gain an advantage through deception.

In 1900, the wording of U.S. Navy Regulations was changed to state that no action or battle shall be undertaken without first displaying the national ensign. The flying of a false color was omitted and never mentioned again in subsequent revisions. All warships of the U.S. Navy were required to display the national flag before firing a shot in battle during World War II. Even on submarines that surfaced quickly to engage an enemy vessel, the ensign had to be hoisted before a deck gun went into action.

The current U.S. Navy Regulations, 1972 edition with revisions, states that the U.S. ensign shall be displayed during battle. The ensign is now flown continuously during wartime, since battle is always imminent.

* * *

TWENTIETH-CENTURY ARMOR

All U.S. combat troops in Korea were equipped with a type of body armor before the war ended.

The revival of body armor, after a lapse of several centuries, was made possible by twentieth-century plastics. Nylon pads and thin slabs of Fiberglass were combined in a sleeveless vest weighing about eight and a half pounds and allowing freedom of movement. The armor was capable of stopping .45-calibre automatic pistol bullets, submachine gun slugs, and most shell, mortar, or grenade fragments of a velocity less than 1,100 feet per second.

On the basis of U.S. Army and Marine Corps surveys, it was established that body armor prevented 60 to 70 percent of chest and abdominal wounds, while reducing the severity of 25 to 30 percent of the wounds resulting from penetrations. Aside from humanitarian aspects, this meant that a large proportion of the enemy's most effective antipersonal weapons were rendered useless. The result, according to U.S. infantry officers in Korea, was a marked increase in combative spirit.

* * *

OLD SOLDIER WINTER

Weather has much to do with warfare. This was especially true in the high North Korean plateau. There during their breakout from the Chinese trap at Chosin

Reservoir, the American Marines were compelled to run the engines of their vehicles every hour to keep them from freezing. The hard earth there was often too hard to dig foxholes, barricades were often made of frozen bodies; and men often freed their frozen rifle bolts by urinating on them.

*   *   *

"I'VE BEEN AROUND THE WORLD IN A PLANE . . ."

In 1957, three U.S. Air Force jets took off from an airport in California, flew around the earth, and returned to the same airport from which they had taken off. The entire flight was completed in just 45 hours and 19 minutes, a record for the shortest round-the-world flight in history. The total distance each of the three jets traveled was 24,325 miles.

*   *   *

A HALF BAKED COURT-MARTIAL

At one of the strangest Army trials on record, a private was court-martialed for peeling potatoes improperly.

PFC Andrew God, Jr., was accused of the deed while on KP duty at Fort Myer, Va. Instead of digging the eyes out with the point of his knife in a proper manner, God hacked the eyes of the spuds off.

A large portion of the potatoes were wasted, said his captain and the mess sergeant, and God was charged with having "willfully suffered potatoes of some value, the military property of the United States, to be destroyed by improper peeling."

God pleaded guilty at his trial in 1959. "You can't jab a potato with a knife and dig into it," he said. "If the knife slips, you've got it in your hand." Part of his lawyer's defense was to prove that a month's worth of God's potato peelings—saved in a large pan—weighed less than those of his mess sergeant.

In the end justice prevailed and the charges were "repealed."

* * *

FALLING INTO THE WILD BLUE YONDER WITHOUT A PARACHUTE

"The world's biggest step" was inscribed on the cockpit door of the balloon. How prophetic these words were! For the balloon carrying Joseph Kittinger, a United States Air Force captain, was 19 miles in the sky, sailing along at a height of 102,000 feet over New Mexico, when on August 16, 1960, Kittinger took a step and made history.

Kittinger picked up speed each second as he fell freely through the air. His parachute was packed firmly on his back as he fell mile after mile. He encountered a pitiless wind as he reached a falling speed of over 600 miles an hour. Yet the 32-year-old Kittinger maintained his composure even though at times the air temperature was as low as 94 degrees below zero.

The dauntless captain dropped 84,700 feet—more than 16 miles—before releasing his chute! He had fallen through space for four minutes and 38 seconds, a world's record for a free fall.

It took Kittinger 13 minutes to float down the last three miles to terra firm after he finally opened his parachute.

* * *

IF IT MOVES, SALUTE IT

In an effort to maintain military discipline "in and out of uniform" during the last days of the American presence in Vietnam, Major Paul M. Boseman, operations officer of the 377th Security Police Squad, issued the following order: "Salute when you recognize an officer, even though you both, officer and non-commissioned officer, are nude."

* * *

ON VIETNAM

"No sane person in the country likes the war in Vietnam, and neither does President Johnson."—Hubert H. Humphrey (in a televised statement).

* * *

FIRST BROTHER AND SISTER GENERALS

Elizabeth Paschel Hoisington of Newton, Kansas, was sworn in on June 11, 1970, as a brigadier general. Her brother Perry Milo Hoisington, had been made a brigadier general in March, 1958. Their two brothers and their father were also officers.

* * *

MOST BOMBED COUNTRY

The most heavily bombed country in modern times has been Laos. It has been estimated that between May

1964 and February 26, 1973, some 2½ million tons of bombs of all kinds were dropped along the North to South Ho Chi Minh Trail supply route to South Vietnam.

* * *

HE FOUNDED HIS OWN COUNTRY

A former British major named Roy Bates moved in 1966 with his wife and son to a 10-by-25-foot cement caisson that had been built seven miles off the British coast during World War II.

Bates named the platform "Sealand" and declared it to be an independent country. He crowned himself king and his wife queen, designed passports, issued postage stamps, and even created a Sealand dollar.

Today Sealand is the world's smallest country, and King Roy still reigns. They are beyond the three-mile limit and Bates and his kingdom are outside the jurisdiction of any other country.

* * *

LADY BIRD'S LEAST FAVORITE GENERAL

The Department of the Interior informed First Lady Lady Bird Johnson that the first beneficiary of a gift for monument-cleaning in Washington, D.C., would be the statue of General Sherman.

"Does it have to be General Sherman?" she asked. "He's my least favorite general." Told that it had to be Sherman, because his statue was the dirtiest and most in need of cleaning, she said in a resigned voice, "Well, let's go ahead and clean him up, but let's just don't announce it."

*   *   *

QUIET, PLEASE!

In 1972 physicians at the Walter Reed Army Medical Center estimated that of the more than 500,000 men who were receiving military combat training, more than half would sustain permanent hearing loss due to the noise of the weaponry.

*   *   *

NIXON'S HIGH FLYING DEMOCRACY KITS

Thousands of "Democracy Kits" were dropped over North Vietnam in 1972 by the Committee to Re-elect the President. The kits consisted of brooches and handsome pen-and-pencil sets—the latter decorated with the presidential seal and the signature of Richard Nixon. The pen-and-pencil sets were the kind presented to generous political contributors. They had been left over from the campaign.

*   *   *

THE STRANGE CASE OF THE MISSING MUSKET PARTS

In December, 1973, Dan Campanelli of Oakland, New Jersey, was given a Civil War musket as a gift. The musket was in good condition except for a few missing parts. Dan searched to no avail for a trigger, trigger guard, and metal screw. Finally he heard about a gun club and went to the very next meeting. Dan met a man there selling antique gun parts. The salesman looked at Dan's musket and said he was positive he had no parts for it. While the salesman talked, Dan picked up a trigger guard, trigger, and metal screw. When he tried them out on the stock, they fell right into place. The man selling parts was amazed, especially since the parts Dan needed were the only parts he had for that particular type of gun.

"These guns are made of hand-forged iron and hand-carved wood," the man explained, "and among identical weapons the parts are usually not interchangeable. You must have found the parts from your own gun."

* * *

STIFF PRICE FOR A PIE IN THE EYE

Naval history was made when Seabee Leon L. Louie became the first person ever to be court-martialed for pie throwing. A slapstick plan was devised by a group of bored sailors at Port Hueneme, California, "to boost morale." Luckless Louie volunteered to do the pitching.

Winding up his pitching arm, Louie withdrew a chocolate cream pie from a paper bag and squashed it in the face of Chief Warrant Officer Timothy P. Curtain.

Curtain was not amused. In December, 1974, Louie was brought to trial. Louie's attorney went so far as to call the comedian Soupy Sales as an expert for the defense. Soupy testified that he had been on the receiving end of "more than 10,000 [pies] since 1950. It's the thing you can really do to relieve tension without hurting anybody."

* * *

THE ARMY'S FIRST WOMAN PARACHUTIST

In 1978, at age 22, Cheryl Stearns became the first woman parachutist of the U.S. Army's official parachute team, the Golden Knights.

Stearns has broken a number of records, some of which were held by the Russian women's parachute team. She has nearly doubled the existing world records for day and night accuracy jumping by hitting a four-inch target on the ground after leaping from 2,500 feet up. She scored 43 consecutive hits during the day and 23 at night.

In June, 1978, at the National Parachuting Championships in Richmond, Indiana, she won the women's events in the individual style and accuracy competition.

She set a world record in the style event with a time of 6.4 seconds to gain the U.S. women's title.

What parachutists call "style" is jumping from more than 6,000 feet up and doing a series of timed free-fall rolls and turns.

The attractive Cheryl, who borrowed $40 from her mother to make her first parachute jump, plans to be a jet pilot when she leaves the Army.

* * *

SLOW-MOTION DIPLOMACY

On August 15, 1978, 33 years after V-J Day, China and Japan signed a "peace and friendship" treaty, formally ending their part in World War II. But there has yet to be a formal peace treaty between Germany and the Soviet Union.

* * *

BELLICOSE BELLES

Although the law bars women from specialties likely to involve close combat, on January 24, 1980, more than half of 62 female graduates of West Point Military Academy chose combat branches.

* * *

YOU'VE COME A LONG WAY, BABY

The job of mercenary soldier is no longer for men only. The August, 1981, issue of *Soldier of Fortune* magazine printed an ad from a 28-year-old female mercenary seeking work. The ad stated in part, "Thorough and discreet, sophisticated 1981 equipment. I prefer a one-woman job. No team projects. I have done undercover surveillance and bodyguard work. Will travel. I am strictly professional and command top $$$$."

* * *

THE COST OF DEFENSE

The estimated level of spending on armaments throughout the world in 1981 was $640 billion. This represents $140 per person per year, or more than 9 percent of the world's total production of goods and services. In 1981 it was estimated that there were 23.2 million full-time armed forces regulars or conscripts.

The budgeted expenditure on defense by the U.S. government in the year ending June 30, 1982, was $171,023 million or 5.7 percent of the country's gross national product. For the financial year 1982, this was raised to $185.8 billion.

The defense burden on the USSR has been variously estimated at a percentage of GNP to be greater than 15 percent by China, up to 14 percent by Britain and up to 13 percent by the CIA, and thus may be nearly three times that of the U.S.

* * *

OLDEST FEMALE MILITARY VETERAN

In 1983, an Indiana woman, believed to be the nation's oldest female military veteran, got a treat for her 100th birthday—a congratulatory letter from President Reagan. Pearl Love of Osgood, Indiana, a veteran of World War I, said she remembers shaking hands with Woodrow Wilson and seeing Teddy Roosevelt once in a parade.

* * *

THE VIETNAM ERA'S UNKNOWN SOLDIER

The Arlington National Cemetery had tombs of the Unknown Soldiers from both world wars and the Korean conflict. But it wasn't until 1984 that an Unknown Soldier killed in the Vietnam war was buried there.

In 1973, Congress directed the Pentagon to select an unknown Vietnam-era serviceman. Military identification had become so sophisticated, from fingerprints to X-ray records for tooth fillings, that there were no unknown soldiers who might be candidates for the tomb. It was 11 years before a body could be found that met the four criteria set out in the law. Those four standards were that he was an American, a serviceman, he died in battle, and he was unidentified.

* * *

SAFE EXPLOSIVE

A Japanese firm, Nippon Oils and Fats Co., has developed a safe explosive. Urbanite demolishes rock, concrete, and steel with very little noise and less violence. Urbanite is so safe that it can be detonated at rush hour in the middle of a busy city without threat to life or limb.

A spokesman for the company says the secret is urbanite's slowness to burn. The main ingredient is nitroglycerin but several secret ingredients have been added to reduce its burning speed to about a fourth of dynamite and the resultant noise to about one-third that of a jack hammer. But the bad news is that the price is about four times that of dynamite.

* * *

THERE IS NO CONGRESSIONAL MEDAL OF HONOR

There is no such medal as the Congressional Medal of Honor. The nations highest award for bravery is officially the Medal of Honor. But since it is presented "in the name of the Congress of the United States," the public has choosen to include the term Congressional.

* * *

WORLD'S LARGEST VEHICLE

The longest vehicle in the world is the U.S. Army overland train. The truck is 572 feet long—almost 1/10 mile! It is used to transport rockets or other very long objects, weighs 450 tons, and has 54 wheels, four engines and a 7,828-gallon fuel capacity.

*   *   *

AWoL

The military abbreviation for *Absent Without Leave*, should technically be abbreviated AWL. But the U.S. War Department, apprehensive that AWL would be misconstrued as *Absent With Leave*, inserted the O, despite the fact that without is one word.

*   *   *

"MOM"

According to the Recruitment Code of the U.S. Navy, anyone "bearing an obscene and indecent" tattoo will be rejected.

*   *   *

SLEEP TIGHT

The military custom of sounding taps before lights out originated in public houses. Drinkers were alerted that the tap room was about to close for the night by a signal known as "taps-up."

*   *   *

STAND FOR THE NATIONAL ANTHEM

In the United States all persons are expected to rise and stand during a rendition of "The Star-Spangled Banner," the nation's legally adopted national anthem.

The custom of standing to express loyalty, particularly when the national anthem is sung or being played, is a survival of an ancient military practice. It was customary during the Middle Ages for everybody present to stand while any kind of military or patriotic demonstration was taking place. The practice is related in origin to the custom that forbids an inferior to sit down in the presence of a superior until told to do so.

* * *

NEW FOWL WEAPON

A new weapon was recently proclaimed by the *Chemical and Engineering News.* The weapon, a pneumatic cannon, can fire dead chickens at speeds up to 620 miles per hour. This fowl weapon was devised by the National Research council of Canada to test airplane parts likely to be struck by birds. The cannon will hold either your standard four-pound chicken, for testing windshields, or the sturdy eight-pound chicken, for testing tail assemblies. The big piece of artillery will also fire synthetic chickens.